Maharal
EMERGING PATTERNS

Maharal
EMERGING PATTERNS

TEN REPRESENTATIVE ESSAYS
CULLED FROM THE WORK OF
RABBI YEHUDAH LOEW
OF PRAGUE

YAAKOV ROSENBLATT

FELDHEIM PUBLISHERS
JERUSALEM   NEW YORK

First published 2001

Copyright © 2001
by Yaakov Rosenblatt and Feldheim Publishers

ISBN 1-58330-475-4

All rights reserved.
No part of this publication may be translated, reproduced, stored in a retrieval system or transmitted, in any form or by any means, electronic, mechanical, photocopying, recording, or otherwise, without permission in writing from the publishers.

FELDHEIM PUBLISHERS
POB 35002 / Jerusalem, Israel

202 Airport Executive Park
Nanuet, NY 10954

www.feldheim.com

Printed in Israel

In Loving Memory of
Our Beloved Zaide

ישראל יצחק ב"ר יהודה ז"ל
Mr. Isaac Hamm *z"l*
1913-1999

Born on the Lower East Side at a time when *Yiddishkeit* was in decline, he grew stronger from the challenges that weakened others. A man of determination, with a rock-solid commitment to tradition, he raised a family of *b'nei Torah*, an accomplishment that always made him proud.

His strength and vigor will forever be an inspiration to his family and those who knew him. He will always be missed.

ת.נ.צ.ב.ה.

MAHARAL INSTITUTE
RABBI PINCHOS GRUMAN
DEAN

מכון מהר"ל
הרב פנחס גרומן
מנהל

I was once told by the Bostoner Rebbe, *zt"l*, that the difference between Maharal and Ramchal (Rabbi Moshe Chaim Luzzatto) is that while Ramchal plucks objects from Heaven and places them on the ground, Maharal picks objects from the ground and places them in Heaven.

Maharal's work is the foundation of much of Jewish thought today. It is the intellectual base of both *Chassidus* and *Mussar*. The *chassidim* of Gur, Alexander, and Sochotchov comprised the majority of observant Jews that lived in pre-World War II Poland. The originator of those dynasties was Rabbi Simcha Bunim of P'shischa. He is often quoted to have said: "No one can possibly understand *chassidus* without learning Maharal."

In Galicia, the Sanzer Rebbe in his commentary to the Torah, *Divrei Chaim*, quotes Maharal continuously and extensively. In Russia, the first Lubavitcher Rebbe writes in the introduction to his classic, *Tanya*, that his work is based on "*sofrim* and *seforim*"; *seforim* referring to the works of Maharal of Prague.

Closer to our times, the late Satmar Rebbe, *zt"l*, often said before Pesach: "How can we approach the Seder without first studying Maharal's *Gevuros Hashem*?"

On the *Litvish* side of the spectrum, Rabbi Eliyahu Dessler, the famed Mashgiach of Yeshivos Gateshead and Ponevezh, often develops themes of the Maharal, albeit in the language of *Mussar*. Rare is the Mashgiach or Rosh Yeshiva today who does not quote Maharal in addressing his *talmidim* or others.

A CHALLENGING WORK

The Maharal's *seforim* are difficult to understand for at least four reasons.

(1) His thought patterns are unique and novel. He seldom quotes anyone else; his sources are almost always *Chazal* – and *Chazal* alone. His thought patterns are not a continuation of anyone else's line of thinking. Consequently, one can not prepare himself to learn his works.

(2) Maharal's writings are beyond simple classification: They are not Kabbalah, yet there is a significant element of Kabbalah within them. They are not Torah exegeses, yet there is a significant amount of Torah exegeses within them. They are not philosophy, yet there is a significant element of philosophy within them. Indeed, they are all of the above, yet none of the above exclusively.

(3) To accommodate his novel thought, Maharal creates a terminology all his own. Terms like *nivdal* and *hasagah* are invested with meanings unique to his writings alone. Yet, he will often slip back to the conventional meaning of those words in his writings.

(4) Maharal is monistic in his *weltanschauung*. Unlike many others, he explains that the physical appearance of a person or an item and its character, relate to its spiritual essence. Even the punctuation and spelling of an item's name, as well as its geographical and temporal position, are descriptions of its essence.

THIS BOOK

Rabbi Yaakov Rosenblatt, an accomplished scholar, has mastered the works of Maharal: the rigor of his thought, his subtle nuances, broad patterns, and minutiae of language and style. His work does not translate Maharal; it extrapolates his essential ideas and renders them lucid and available to readers who, while not scholars in Maharal, have intense intellectual curiosity.

Rabbi Rosenblatt's *Maharal: Emerging Patterns* is a gigantic step towards understanding Maharal. He has succeeded at culling patterns of Torah philosophy from Maharal's writings, and makes them accessible to the English reader. He does so without sacrificing the depth of Maharal. Instead, he intrigues the reader for more.

Respectfully,

HaRav Pinchos Gruman

DATA — AN EXCEPTIONAL JEWISH LEARNING EXPERIENCE.

BS"D
Rosh Chodesh Shevat, 5761
Dallas, Texas

RABBI YERACHMIEL D. FRIED
Dean
RABBI BENTZI EPSTEIN
Director
RABBI YEHUDAH ABRAMS
Administrative Director

RABBINICAL FACULTY
RABBI RANAAN BRODERICK
RABBI SHMUEL HERSKOVITS
RABBI YISROEL KATZ
RABBI MENACHEM MOZES
RABBI YAAKOV ROSENBLATT
RABBI NESANYA ZAKON

ZAMIRA RAICHGOD
Office Manager

OFFICERS
RICHARD GLAZER
President
OSCAR ROSENBERG
Vice-President Fundraising
RICHARD SOLOMAN
Treasurer
JOSEPH ROTHSTEIN, M.D.*
Secretary

UNIQUELY OURS
DATA's WOMEN'S DIVISION
PATTY GOLDSCHMIEDT
SUSAN HERSH
Co-Presidents

BOARD MEMBERS
WARREN ABRAMS
JOSEPH BENPORAT
STEVE BOCK
RUMIE BURSTEIN
KENNY BROODO
BRIAN COHEN, M.D.
STEVE COHEN, M.D.
CAL DONSKY
RIVKA GEDALIA
ARIELA GOLDSTEIN
JAMIE HAYDEN
NORMAN HOPPENSTEIN
LAWRENCE KOSOWSKY*
YURI LEMESHEV, M.D.
PETER LESSER
MARSHALL LESTZ
LIZ LIENER
ELIOT LITOFF
SOL LURIE, M.D.
LOWELL MICHELSON
LIORA PEISER, PHD
HAROLD PINKER
ALAN PRESS
ARI REUBEN
WENDY RICHKER
BERNIE ROSENBERG
JO-ANN SAUNDERS
JEREMY SCHARF
ALLAN SHULKIN, M.D.
FREDELL SHULKIN
SUSAN TURNER
LINDA TYCHER
DAVID WEINER
HARVEY WEINER
MAX WILDER
DAVID WISEMAN, PHD
DAVID WOHLSTADTER*
MIKE ZUCKER

PAST PRESIDENTS

"The Torah of Hashem is perfect, restoring the soul... making the simple one wise... gladdening the heart... enlightening the eyes... enduring forever...." (Psalms 19) The power of the Torah to affect the soul so profoundly is realized when one plumbs the depths of its meaning. Generations of Jews and countless souls have been lost to our nation because they received only a superficial understanding of Torah. They were led to mistakenly believe that Toras Hashem lacks depth and meaning, Heaven forbid.

For hundreds of years the writings of Maharal of Prague have accomplished just that: they have revealed the inner beauty, depth, and profundity of every word and letter of our holy Torah. Once exposed to Maharal's teachings, one knows forever that the Torah is "Toras Chaim," a living Torah, one that "gladdens the heart, enlightens the eyes, and endures forever."

Yet, Maharal's teachings have remained a "closed book" for our brothers and sisters who are as of yet not acquainted with the intricacies of Torah, the Hebrew language and its nuances. For this we owe a dept of gratitude to our dear friend and colleague, Rabbi Yaakov Rosenblatt, for toiling tirelessly to unlock the mysteries of many of Maharal's concepts for the English reader. I have read this impressive work and found that he has touched on many critical points of Jewish philosophy.

We at the Dallas Kollel feel very fortunate and honored to have a scholar of the caliber of Rabbi Rosenblatt, a graduate of Beth Medrash Govoha of Lakewood, NJ - Lakewood NJ, as a member of our Beis Hamedrash. It is our prayer that this important work, *"Maharal: Emerging Patterns,"* as well as his future works, will enlighten the eyes of countless Jews to the beauty, depth and truth of Torah, hastening the arrival of Mashiach Tzidkeinu, Bimheira Viyameinu.

Respectfully,

Yerachmiel D. Fried
Rabbi Yerachmiel D. Fried, Rosh HaKollel
Author, *Yom Tov Sheini Kehilchaso*

DALLAS AREA TORAH ASSOCIATION / COMMUNITY KOLLEL
5840 FOREST LANE DALLAS, TX 75230 TEL: 214.987.DATA (3282) FAX: 214.987.1764
EMAIL: DATA@DATANET.ORG WEB: WWW.DATANET.ORG

Acknowledgments

While writing may be the pursuit of the individual, publishing is an effort that cannot be accomplished without the dedication of many.

I would like to thank Rabbi Avraham Chaim Carmell for his scholarly and lucid Introduction on the Maharal.

I am grateful to R' Yaakov Feldheim for his interest in publishing this book and to the members of his editorial, design, and production staff at Feldheim Publishers in Jerusalem for their professional work. Mrs. Joyce Bennett directed the production of this book. My editor, Mrs. Deena Nataf, gave the writing fluency and charge. Mrs. Bracha Steinberg's attractive design enhanced the book's appearance.

Indeed, I am indebted not only to those who have helped the publication process, but also to those who inspired me to embark on the project.

My parents, Rabbi and Mrs. Zev Rosenblatt, have given me more than I can ever acknowledge. The have nurtured and encouraged me throughout my life. I thank them for everything.

My in-laws, Rabbi and Mrs. Eliyahu Stewart of Los Angeles, have raised a family that is admired and respected. The more I get to know them, the more I come to understand why. Marrying into their beautiful family was the best decision that I have ever made.

My Roshei Yeshivos and Rabbeim — at RJJ, Edison NJ; Mir, Yerushalayim; and Beth Medrash Govoha, Lakewood, NJ — have guided and inspired me from childhood to the present. I will always be inspired by their lesson.

Perhaps most pivotal in my development were my rebbeim,

Perhaps most pivotal in my development were my rebbeim, HaRav Naftali Kaplan, *shlita*, and HaRav Chaim Yitzchok Kaplan, *shlita*. They showed me all that I can be and inspired me to try to get there. I will forever be grateful for their warmth and example.

Rabbi Yerachmiel Fried, the Rosh Kollel of the Dallas Area Torah Association in which I study, has helped develop an amazing Torah network in that city. I am privileged to be able to study under him.

Humbly, I thank HaRav Pinchos Gruman, *shlita*, Rosh M'chon Maharal and Rav D'Kehal Beis Naftali of Los Angeles, who has studied Maharal with me during the *bein hazemanim* periods I spent in that city. His mastery of Maharal and lifelong dedication to its study continue to inspire me.

My first *chavrusa* for Maharal was Rabbi Moshe Haikins of Lakewood, NJ. Without a doubt, it was he who got me "on board." His friendship is one that I cherish, and his insights have helped me greatly.

Kudos to Rabbi Tzvi Black for publishing my first notes on Maharal on his website, JewishAmerica.com. Rabbi Black is an *oseik b'tzarchei tzibur*, who is bringing *emunah* to our Jewish brethren every single day.

As I come to the end of this list, I know that I must now thank my dear wife Suri. Language is inadequate to express my feelings. Her sole desire is for my spiritual growth and for our children to be raised as *b'nei Torah*. All I can say is that I am indebted to her in a most essential way.

Finally, I thank the Creator of the world for giving me the inspiration to begin this project and the peace of mind to complete it. And I thank Him, most of all, for allowing my family to be part of His glorious people, *Am Yisrael*. It is an experience that studying and writing Maharal has brought me to understand and appreciate ever more deeply.

Yaakov Rosenblatt
Dallas, Texas
Teves 5761

Preface

Long before I even knew what the acronym "Maharal" meant, I revered his work. My rabbis imprinted that reverence onto me. Their eyes danced when they studied his works, and their spirits soared when they taught them to us. And that is why, years later, when I wanted to study a philosophical Jewish text, Maharal was the natural choice. About three years ago a friend and I initiated a learning session to study *Tiferes Yisrael*, one of the Maharal's most famous books.

The work affected me greatly. Maharal challenges our assumptions about Torah concepts. He asks difficult questions and presents complicated challenges. Then he resolves them. Often, he will pull a single strand out of a question and develop it until it takes on a more complicated form. When it is thus replaced into the original "fabric," a new pattern is revealed. The question is undone, and the wisdom of Torah is revealed at a deeper level. Maharal searches for truth, and his writings take you along on his journey.

It would be beyond my ability to present a full presentation of the wisdom of Maharal. Instead, I have attempted to chart out a number of his questions, to present his answers, and then to explain, to some degree, the chain of thought that brought him there.

As this is a presentation and not a translation of Maharal, I have often added examples and background information to elucidate difficult points. Each essay is also accompanied by a footnote to direct the reader to the source in Maharal's original Hebrew works. Each of the book's ten chapters contains a collection of thought on a specific topic. With one exception, they are all culled from Maharal's works *Tiferes Yisrael* and *Gevuros Hashem*.

Maharal has brought me to see undercurrents in areas of Torah that had previously seemed calm, and great foundations in areas that had appeared to be piles of stones. It has sent me on a journey to probe deeper, to ask more, and to always search for the next level.

If this work, in some small way, brings others to do the same, it will have served its purpose entirely.

Contents

Preface. *11*
Introduction: The Maharal MiPrague,
        by Rabbi Avraham Chaim Carmell . *15*
1: Avraham *37*
2: Bris Bein Habesarim. *47*
3: Yosef. *61*
4: The Ten Plagues *69*
5: The Exodus *77*
6: Sinai *83*
7: The Ten Commandments *93*
8: Torah and Mitzvos *109*
9: The Haggadah *121*
10: Maharal on Hallel. *151*

Introduction: The Maharal MiPrague
by Rabbi Avraham Chaim Carmell

The great city of Prague has been graced by many of the most famous names in Jewish history. The *Levush* and the *Shelah HaKadosh*, the *Tosafos Yom Tov* and the *Kli Yakar*, the *Urim VeTumim* and the *Noda BiYehudah* are just a few of the Torah luminaries who lived in Prague at some point in their lives.

However, the one Torah giant whose name is invariably connected with that beautiful city is the Maharal MiPrague — Rabbi Yehudah Loew ben Rabbi Betzalel, whose towering stature gave direction and prestige to the Jews of Prague for almost thirty years.

An indication of the high esteem in which the Maharal was held by even the non-Jewish residents of Prague is the large statue erected in his honor outside the new city hall, built in 1917, three hundred years after the Maharal passed away.

As children we read about the wondrous ways in which the Maharal saved his brethren from the evil plans of their enemies. Particularly captivating are the legends about Yossele the *Golem* — a man formed out of clay that the Maharal is purported to have created to protect the Jews of Prague.* And as adults we often

---

* These legends first appeared in a book published in 1909 in Pietritrov. They are almost certainly fictitious since no mention whatsoever is made of the *golem* in earlier works that refer to the Maharal, including *Tzemach David*, written by a student of the Maharal, and *Megillas Yuchsin*, written by a grandson!

hear quotes from the Maharal's deep insights into the aggadic statements of *Chazal*.

As a result, the Maharal has a certain mystical aura connected with his name. This makes it difficult to envisage his true position as a dynamic leader who stood in the forefront of European Jewish life for over half a century.

Chazal tell us that when studying the teachings of a Torah sage, one should "imagine the author standing before him." The following account of what is known about the life and activities of the Maharal MiPrague will help the student of his teachings form a picture of who this great teacher was and why he was viewed even during his lifetime as "that pillar of iron that the entire House of Israel relies upon" (The *Tosafos Yom Tov* — Rabbi Yom Tov Lipman Heller).

Early Years

The sixteenth century is commonly accepted as the beginning of the era of the *Acharonim* (later commentators). Major works that left a lasting imprint on Torah literature were authored during this century. This is the period when the *Shulchan Aruch* by Rabbi Yosef Karo combined with the glosses of the Rema, Rabbi Moshe Isserlis, became the accepted code of Jewish law. The Maharshal, Rabbi Shlomo Luria and the Maharsha, Rabbi Shmuel Eidelis authored their commentaries which are to be found at the back of almost every edition of the Talmud. In Tzefas, the holy Arizal, Rabbi Yitzchak Luria, revealed new worlds of Kabbalistic insights to his student Rabbi Chaim Vital.

It was into this period, about twenty years after the expulsion of the Jews from Spain, that the Maharal was born in the town of Posen, which then belonged to Poland.

His father, Reb Betzalel, was the oldest of three brothers, sons of Reb Chaim of Worms, Germany. Reb Betzalel's brothers were sent to Poland to learn Torah at the yeshivah of the Maharshal, while he remained behind to take care of their aging father. When his brothers returned after a number of years as accomplished *talmidei chachamim* (Torah scholars), Betzalel voiced his regret and disappointment at having been denied the same opportunity. His father consoled him with a blessing that he would have four sons who would illuminate the world with their Torah.

This blessing came true, and Reb Betzalel's four sons were great — each in his own right. The oldest, Reb Chaim, was a colleague of the Rema and authored a number of *sefarim*. He served as chief rabbi of Worms.

The second son, Reb Sinai, had a yeshivah in Prague and later served as chief rabbi of Nikolsburg and all of Moravia. The third son, Reb Shimshon, was chief rabbi of Kremnitz. His daughter was the mother of the great kabbalist, Rabbi Shimshon of Ostropolia.

The youngest son of Reb Betzalel, and by far the most famous, was Yehudah Loew, known to us as the Maharal.

According to the family records, the Maharal was born in 5272/1512. According to one legend, he was born on the first night of Pesach. Members of the household, who rushed out to call a midwife, scared off a local peasant who was about to deposit a corpse in Reb Betzalel's basement in order to instigate a blood-libel. Thus his very entrance into this world was a portent of the many instances that he would save his brethren from calamity [as mentioned on his tombstone].

Little is known of where the Maharal received his early education. He refers to his teachers very infrequently, and never mentions them by name. It is very likely that he did not study under any great *rosh yeshivah* and spent his formative years studying in the local *battei midrash* developing his Talmudic prowess through group study. When he came to Prague in his later years, he established a *beis midrash* on these lines, and in his writings, he extols the method of group discussion as the way to acquire objective thinking.

When discussing his oft-stated opinions on the correct methodology of Torah study, he bemoans the fact that in his youth he indulged in the *pilpul* approach to Talmudic analysis that dominated Eastern European Torah centers for many centuries. However, from his works it is apparent that he also studied *Tanach* (Scriptures), Hebrew grammar, philosophy, and Kabbalah.

When he reached marriageable age, the Maharal became engaged to Perl, the daughter of one of the wealthiest and most influential residents of Prague known as "Reich Shmelke" (Shmelke the Rich). His future father-in-law promised to support the couple in order to enable the Maharal to continue his studies.

However, shortly after the engagement, Reich Shmelke lost all his wealth as a result of false libels that were leveled at the Jews of Prague and their subsequent expulsion by King Ferdinand. Their property and possessions were plundered and, as a result, even when they were allowed to return a few years later, "Reich Shmelke" was left quite penniless.

He wrote to the Maharal, freeing him from his commitment to marry his daughter. But the sensitive Maharal would not consider breaking off the engagement and expressed his readiness to wait until the family would be in a position to arrange the wedding. Meanwhile, Perl supported her parents by selling bread and cakes.

One day a soldier rode by and snatched one of her loaves. She grabbed hold of his horse's bridle and insisted that he pay for the bread. The soldier promised that he would return to pay for it and, as a guarantee, left her his cloak. When he didn't return, Perl examined the cloak and found it lined with golden ducats. She immediately wrote to the Maharal, informing him that she was ready to get married. The wedding took place in 5304/1544. The Maharal was thirty-two years old by then, and his wife was twenty-eight. They were blessed with six daughters and one son, whom they named Betzalel after the Maharal's father.

First Public Office

It is not known whether the Maharal settled in Prague after his wedding, or remained in Posen. Nine years later, in 1553, he was elected to his first public office as chief rabbi of Nikolsburg and all of Moravia.

For twenty years the Maharal guided and taught his flock, who became very attached to him. Even after he left for Prague, they continued to turn to him for advice, referring to him as their teacher and leader.

This endearment was not just a reflection of his elevated stature as a giant in Torah and his unique presentation of the ethical teachings of *Chazal*. The Maharal was a leader in the broader sense of the word. With his clear, organized way of thinking, he introduced a new order into the communal life of the Jewish communities under his jurisdiction.

The collection of laws and regulations of the Moravian communities attributed to him contains detailed guidelines for the fair election of city councils, collection of charity and taxes, and limits on the ostentatious show of dress and jewelry. Shortly before he left Moravia, he was asked to render a similar service to the community of Londenburg.

His success in this area was recognized far and wide, and many years after he left Moravia, the community of Proznitz turned to him to draft for them a similar set of community rules, which he did in 1583.

The Maharal also took steps to eradicate the laxity that had crept into two areas of mitzvah observance. The first was the prohibition against drinking non-Jewish wine, which he found was being flagrantly disregarded by many Jews — particularly the more well-to-do. The second was the habit of talking in the synagogue during prayers and the reading from the Torah.

His efforts in these two areas, which he mentions in his writings, culminated in the institution of two *mi-she'berach* prayers that were to be read out in all synagogues after the reading of the Torah. These prayers, which contained blessings for those who were careful in such matters, served as a weekly reminder of the severity of the issues concerned. The prayer concerning not talking during prayers was reinstituted after the terrible massacres during the Chemelincki uprising of 1648–9 (known as *Tach VeTat*) by the Maharal's great student, the *Tosafos Yom Tov*, and is now referred to as the *Tosafos Yom Tov*'s *mi-she'berach*.

Prague

After twenty years of productive work as the chief rabbi of Moravia, the Maharal left this highly respected position and moved to Prague in Bohemia. The reasons for this decision are not clear. Perhaps the Maharal, who was not financially dependent on his position, wished to direct his energies towards teaching his unique method of Torah study and producing his even more novel literary works in which he presents his innovative approach to understanding the aggadic teachings of *Chazal*.

So it was in the year 1573 that the Maharal took up residence in Prague as a private individual. Prague was at that time under the able leadership of Chief Rabbi Yitzchak Melnick, who maintained a yeshivah and was actively involved in the charitable organizations of the community.

Shortly after his arrival, the Maharal established himself in the newly built "Klaus" synagogue. This synagogue had been built as a tribute to the Emperor Maximillian II who, two years previously, had graced the Jewish residents of Prague with a royal visit to their ghetto.

The Maharal's concept of a *beis midrash* was a learning environment wherein each individual gained his own mastery over large sections of Talmudic literature while developing and sharpening his understanding through group discussion. The *shiurim* (lectures) he gave demonstrated how a clear analysis of the Talmud enabled the student to arrive at the correct halachic conclusion.

This was a sharp deviation from the standard method of Talmudic study popular at the time. Most yeshivos followed the method of *pilpul* developed by Rabbi Yaakov Pollack, also of Prague (d. 1530). This consisted of an exacting analysis of the commentaries of the *Tosafos* printed in all editions of the Talmud. Much attention was paid to every nuance of the wording used by the *Tosafos* and new ideas were developed by bringing together far-flung sources to resolve his ideas.

The Maharal waged a lifelong battle against this method. He argued for a more systematic approach that focused on a clear grasp of the content of the Talmudic discussion followed through with the commentaries of the Rif and the Rosh who discuss the halachic conclusions derived from the Talmud. In fact, he wrote that he would have preferred to see the Rosh printed alongside the Gemara and the *Tosafos* at the back.

As part of his policy of gaining a broad knowledge of Talmudic concepts as the basis for Talmudic analysis, he reintroduced the study of *mishnayos* as an independent subject. He encouraged the formation of *mishnayos* groups to study the Mishnah in depth. These soon became popular throughout Europe. His student, Rabbi Yom Tov Lipman Heller, wrote a lengthy commentary on the entire Mishnah that appears in all standard editions of the *mishnayos*.

The Maharal tried to revise elementary education too, with less success. The conventional curriculum of the *chadarim* taught only part of the weekly portion with Rashi, virtually no *mishnayos*, and focused mainly on the Talmud. Talmudic study was begun at a very young age, and after a few years the children were introduced to *Tosafos*.

In his *derashos* (sermons) and writings, the Maharal decried this system as being futile and confusing. He advocated returning to the program outlined in the Mishnah in *Pirkei Avos* (ch. 5), "Scriptures should be taught at five years old, Mishnah at ten, Talmud at fifteen." This way, the child would be introduced to material of increasing complexity according to the development of his intellectual capacity.

He writes that peer pressure and fear of ridicule on the part of the parents stymied all his efforts to effect a change in this area. Yet even in his old age, he continued to express his opposition to what he considered to be a fruitless system that produced ignoramuses.

In 1592, at the age of eighty, he gave a long sermon in Posen on the first day of Shavuos in which he described at length his criticism of the current method of education. He voiced the pain and disappointment he felt at his failure to introduce the reform that he viewed as so vital. He went so far as to issue a call to the youth themselves that they should demand that changes be made.

It was during this period that the idea of a communal burial society — the *Chevrah Kaddisha* — was introduced into Prague by Rabbi Eliezer Ashkenazy who had seen such organizations operating in his native Egypt. Up until this time, arranging a funeral had been a private matter, and the poor were often unable to afford the minimal expenses involved. The Maharal used his great expertise in organizing communal affairs to set forth the rules and practices that form the basis for all subsequent *chevrah kaddisha* associations that have become an integral part of any Jewish community.

First Publications

In 1578, at the age of 66, the Maharal published his first work. This was *Gur Aryeh*, a commentary on Rashi's fundamental interpretation of the *Chumash*. In this work, the Maharal demonstrates three of his basic principles: a) his concise presentation of the Talmud and the Halachah; b) his firm commitment to explaining the Scriptures according to the teachings of the Sages; and, c) his novel approach to understanding the aggadic teachings of the Talmud and the *midrashim*.

Four years later, in 1582, he published his *Gevuras Hashem*. In its seventy-two chapters, he discusses all the aspects of the exile in Egypt and the redemption, including a complete commentary on the Pesach Haggadah. This work was printed anonymously in Poland, partly out of his great humility and possibly for fear of attack from his opponents in Prague. The Maharal's burning dedication to the truth expressed itself in his open criticism of the strife and jealousy that surrounded the appointment to public offices in the Prague community. His outspoken criticism of the *pilpul* method of Rabbi Pollack, who had headed a great yeshivah in Prague, also raised the ire of many of the latter's students, who were counted among the more learned members of the community.

The Maharal therefore might have felt that his innovative approach would be more readily accepted on its own merit in Poland than in his hometown of Prague.

One of the themes developed in this book and repeated in many other works of the Maharal is the unique status of the Jewish people as Hashem's emissaries in the world. During this period, large parts of Europe were under the influence of the fanatical Jesuit priests who launched an all-out attempt to convert Jews to Christianity.

In many cities, Jews were forced to attend the sermons of these priests. Their main message was that God had rejected the Jewish people, and their only hope for salvation was to embrace Christianity. Many Jews would come to hear these diatribes with their ears stuffed with cottonwool!

The Maharal strove to strengthen their awareness of the unique position they held as being Hashem's "firstborn" — the first nation to recognize His sovereignty. His writings also emphasized a complete dedication to the truth of the Mosaic Code of Law as transmitted by *Chazal*. He censors major commentators, such as the Ramban and Ibn Ezra, for deviating from the interpretations of the Talmud and Midrash.

Return to Posen

On the 11th of Iyar 5343/1583, Rabbi Mellnick passed away, and the position of the chief rabbinate of Prague became vacant. The most natural candidate for the office was, of course, the Maharal. He was widely acclaimed as one of the leading *poskim* (deciders of Halachah) in Europe. It was no doubt with this in mind that he was invited to give the *Shabbos Shuvah* sermon, usually delivered by the chief rabbi on the Shabbos between Rosh Hashanah and

Yom Kippur.

The Maharal, always driven by a strong sense of mission and a burning dedication to the truth, had no intention of pandering to the layleaders in whose hands the final decision of his election rested.

In this sermon, which was subsequently published, he elaborated on the evils of the pursuit of fleeting honor. He described in very clear terms how jealousy and pride led people to the most corrupt behavior. Finally, he led into a sharp rebuke concerning the plague of slander and scandal-mongering that was rampant at the time.

It had become almost common practice for people to cast aspersions on the legitimacy of well-known families. Out of jealousy or hatred that resulted from the constant vying for the influential positions in the community, rumors would be circulated that the family-in-question descended from doubtful lineage. In some cases, the charges were no less than claiming that actual incest had occurred.

As preposterous as these stories were, they nevertheless were perpetuated by gossips and tale-mongers, and caused untold embarrassment and damage to many highly respected families. In fact, the Maharal's own family had come under attack, and it was only after the Maharshal personally testified to the distinguished lineage of Rabbi Betzalel, the Maharal's father, that the rumor was quieted.

The catchword for these slanderous tales was the term "nadler." This meant, literally, "birthmark," and was a reference to a case in Posen where two orphans who were about to be married were discovered to be brother and sister as a result of the bride hearing that the groom bore a distinguishing birthmark on his back. Although the tragedy had been averted in that case, the word "nadler" became a byword for children of a forbidden marriage.

After decrying the malicious damage wrought by these scandalous tales, the Maharal called forward ten of the city's leading *rabbanim* and issued a severe ban of excommunication on anyone who used this term in the future.

The entire message of this sermon, in particular his bold action on the "nadler" issue, raised the ire of the community leaders, many of whom suffered these ills that the Maharal had exposed. It is very probable that out of fear that this fearless, outspoken rabbi would undermine their power, the city council decided to elect Rabbi Yitzchak Chaijes as the new chief rabbi of Prague. Rabbi Chaijes, who was a stepbrother of the Maharal's wife, Perl, descended from one of the oldest families in Prague who had been among the founders of the famous Altneushull. He was also a student and proponent of the above-mentioned *pilpul* method taught by Rabbi Yaakov Pollack. The Maharal's sharp condemnation of this method may also have been a factor in the decision to choose his stepbrother-in-law for the position.

Whatever the reason, this appointment was seen by many as a direct affront to the Maharal. It was most likely to prevent any strife his followers might have stirred up that the Maharal chose to return to his hometown of Posen in 1584.

While in Posen, he held a position as one of the town's *rabbanim* and led his own yeshivah. Another famous *rosh yeshivah* in Posen during this period was Rabbi Shmuel Eidelis, the Maharsha.

Back to Prague

Four years later we find the Maharal back in Prague. His brother-in-law, Rabbi Chaijes, found himself unable to navigate the turbulent waters of the internal politics of Prague and was forced to leave Prague for Proznitz in Moravia.

With the reason for his departure no longer relevant, the Maharal submitted to the pressure of his family and students who had remained in Prague, and returned there shortly afterwards.

His sensitive nature did not allow him to accept the position of chief rabbi, now vacated by his stepbrother-in-law's departure.

We find him again, in 1589, giving the sermon normally reserved for the chief rabbi, this time on *Shabbos HaGadol*, the Shabbos preceding Pesach. His topic was how all of creation is unified in its praise of the Creator. He elaborated on the special role the Jewish people play in revealing this unity, and how vital it is that peace and harmony reign among them. In a direct message to the community leaders, he quoted a teaching he had heard in his youth that explained the Torah's juxtaposition of the priestly blessing for peace and the participation of the princes in the inauguration of the Tabernacle (*Bemidbar* 6,7). This is to be seen as an indication to the community leaders that the responsibility of maintaining the peace rests with them.

In the same year, the Maharal published his commentary *Derech Chaim* on *Pirkei Avos*. His brother Rabbi Chaim had died that year, and he no doubt intended the name of the book to be a tribute to him. This is perhaps the most profound of all his works. In it he discusses the relationship of philosophy and Kabbalah, reveals his great insights into human nature, and demonstrates time and again how the seemingly straightforward advice of the Sages reverberates with profound depth that often borders on the esoteric.

Audience with the Emperor

The Maharal's fame spread throughout Prague as the "tall, wise Rabbi Loew of the Jews." He was often visited by Christian scholars, who came to draw on his broad knowledge of religion, philosophy and science. As a result of these discussions, the Kaiser Rudolph II heard about the Maharal's wisdom and asked that he be summoned for an audience. This was a remarkable occurrence, considering the contempt with which the Jew was viewed in the eyes of his Christian neighbors of that time. This encounter is a clear indication of the immense respect and esteem in which the Maharal was held among the academic circles in Prague.

We have a detailed report of the visit written by the Maharal's oldest son-in-law, Rabbi Yitzchak Katz, who accompanied him on the occasion. He gives the date as Sunday, the 23rd of February 1592. He writes how the Maharal was invited to the fortress of Minister Bertier where he was received with great honor and respect. He was led into an inner chamber while his son-in-law and another influential member of the community, who had arranged the meeting, were left in the adjacent room with the door left slightly ajar.

The minister engaged him in a discussion on "esoteric matters," while sitting opposite the Maharal, who was seated on an elegant armchair. Suddenly, there was a scraping of chairs as they rose for the Kaiser, who had stepped into the room from behind a curtain. He joined into the discussion for a short while and then left again.

The Maharal's son-in-law, who heard the entire conversation from where he was sitting, writes that at some opportune time he will reveal the content of the discussion. However, no record has been found. Legends abound about secret information the Maharal revealed to the Kaiser. However, the above firsthand account shows that no attempt was made to conceal the nature of the topic discussed. The most likely conjecture is that the Kaiser, who was deeply involved in medieval alchemy and the occult, had hoped to glean some knowledge on these topics from the Maharal. Whether the Kaiser considered the encounter successful or not is not known. The Maharal's next step put an end to any plans the Kaiser might have had of continuing the relationship.

Back to Posen Again

Shortly after this prestigious audience with the Emperor, the Maharal left Prague for the second time to settle in Posen. As on the previous occasion, it is not clear what prompted this move. Perhaps he wanted to avoid the awkward situation of the Kaiser's requesting that he divulge his knowledge of practical Kabbalah, something the Maharal would have been loathe to do.

His student, Rabbi David Gans, writes in his historical work *Tzemach David*, that the Maharal now held the position of Chief

Rabbi of Poland. Poland was the seat of Torah study and as Chief Rabbi and *Rosh Yeshivah*, the Maharal held hopes that he would be able to put into effect the educational reform he envisaged as described above.

He arrived a few weeks before the festival of Shavuos and, on both days of the Yom Tov, he gave a sermon in the main synagogue. The first, entitled "Discourse on the Torah," is a masterpiece of a rabbinical pulpit sermon. In a skillfully structured presentation, the Maharal sets forth his opinions on the correct method of educating young students to maximize their potential. Although the main topic of his discourse is directed at the Torah students, he did not overlook the problems facing the layman and devoted a section to the role of the Jewish woman.

The second sermon was entitled, "Discourse on the Mitzvos." In it the Maharal traces the development of the Oral Law as an introduction to a harsh criticism of the laxity that existed in neighboring Moravia concerning the rabbinical prohibition against using non-Jewish wine. He concluded with a ban of excommunication on anyone who ordained a rabbi in Moravia who had not proven himself meticulous in this matter. The city of Posen was renowned for its high standard of religious observance. There existed a special seven-member committee that supervised the religious life in the ghetto and ensured that the moral conduct of all the community was in strict accordance with the Torah. The Maharal must have felt that he could rely on the religiously inclined people of Posen to follow his directives and thereby convey the message to the Jews of Moravia that their behavior was unacceptable.

While in Posen, the Maharal published his *Nesivos Olam*. This is a *mussar* work in which he explores "the pathways of commendable character traits," touching on some of the shortcomings of his times.

Chief Rabbi of Prague

The Maharal spent four or five years in Posen, after which he returned to Prague. During these years that the Maharal held the position of chief rabbi in Posen, Rabbi Mordechai Yaffe, author of the *Levushim*, who had been his predecessor, served as chief rabbi of Prague. Now, shortly after the Maharal returned to Prague, Rabbi Yaffe resigned from the rabbinate in Prague and resumed his position in Posen.

It was now, well into his eighties, that the Maharal finally assumed the official position as Chief Rabbi of Prague. Despite his advanced age, he shouldered the full responsibilities as the leader of this leading city in Eastern Europe. His official title was "Chief Rabbi and Dean of the Yeshivah." However, after a year or two, he no longer had the energy to run the yeshivah and suggested that his only son, Rabbi Betzalel, take over this function on his behalf.

Rabbi Betzalel was eminently suitable for the position and his appointment would have been a source of great satisfaction for the Maharal. However, the political intrigue and perpetual internal strife that was so rife in Prague prevented the Maharal from having this dream realized.

A number of the Maharal's close family members held positions of influence in Prague, and it must have been for fear of investing too much power in the hands of one family that the city council refused to accede to the Maharal's request. Instead, they chose Rabbi Efraim Luntshitz, a *darshan* in Prague, to act as the *rosh yeshivah*.

Rabbi Betzalel left Prague as a result and took up a position in Cologne, Germany. The pain caused by his departure turned into tragedy for the Maharal and his wife when Rabbi Betzalel died shortly after this in 1600. His son, Reb Shmuel, remained in Prague and enjoyed a very close relationship with his grandfather.

According to a family legend, the Maharal had bought three plots in the local cemetery for himself, his wife, and his only son Rabbi Betzalel. When Rabbi Betzalel died in Germany, the Maharal promised Reb Shmuel that he would receive this plot.

Shortly before Reb Shmuel passed away, he notified the *chevrah kaddisha* of his grandfather's promise. They claimed that the space available was too narrow for such a large person as Reb Shmuel. He told them to start digging the grave immediately, asking the Maharal to make room for his grandson as he had promised!

By some inexplicable way, the grave diggers were able to dig a normal-sized grave, and when Reb Shmuel died, he was duly buried alongside his grandfather. However, when the time came to lay a tombstone, the place had shrunken to its original size and the family had to make a very tall and narrow headstone.

Final Works

In the two years prior to the tragedy of Rabbi Betzalel's demise, the Maharal produced a spate of books. *Tiferes Yisrael* is devoted to the giving of the Torah at Sinai and discusses the study of Torah and the importance of the practical fulfillment of the mitzvos. This was followed by *Be'er Hagolah*, which can be seen as a sequel to *Tiferes Yisrael*. In it the Maharal tackles many of the challenges leveled at the Oral Law and the teachings of the Sages. He explains many obscure passages in the Talmud and the *midrashim*, and shows how many seemingly incorrect or far-fetched statements contain profound wisdom. *Netzach Yisrael* deals with the issue of the *galus* and the future redemption of the Jewish people. *Or Chadash* and *Ner Mitzvah* discuss the festivals of Purim and Chanukah, respectively.

In his introduction to his major work, *Gevuros Hashem*, the Maharal charts out his plan for a complete series of books. He bases himself on the verse in *Divrei HaYamim* I 29:11, "Yours, Hashem, are the [attributes of] greatness, might, splendor, eternity and glory. For all that is Heaven and earth [is Yours]." The "book of greatness" was to discuss the Shabbos. The "book of might" is *Gevuros Hashem* on Pesach. The "book of splendor" is *Tiferes Yisrael* on Shavuos and the giving of the Torah. The "book of eternity" is *Netzach Yisrael* on Tishah b'Av and the subject of exile and redemption. The fifth was to be the "book of glory" on

Sukkos and the sixth, the "book of Heaven and earth," on Rosh Hashanah and Yom Kippur. Of these, only the second, third and fourth were published. The others were never published and may have never been written.

Another major work of the Maharal remained in manuscript form for over three hundred and fifty years. This is his commentary on the *aggados* of the Talmud which was only recently discovered in the Bodlien Library in Oxford University. The present writer's father, Rabbi Aryeh Carmell, *shlita*, was instrumental in having the original manuscript prepared for publication in 1955. Among the many new ideas are numerous interpretations that can be found in other works of the Maharal, and in one place he writes that he is changing his understanding of a particular statement of the *aggadah*.

Final Years

The Maharal spent his final years in Prague, surrounded by his children and their families and many of his students. In 1604, the Maharal, now over ninety years old, felt that he no longer had the strength to carry the burden of the community and requested to be released from the position of chief rabbi. Rabbi Efraim Luntshitz, who had already taken over his position as *rosh yeshivah*, was now appointed as the official chief rabbi. Although not a direct student of the Maharal, he was a great admirer and agreed with many of his policies. In their petition to the Emperor to authorize the appointment, the city leaders describe the Maharal as old and sickly and in need of much rest. They note that he himself requested permission to resign.

On the 18th of Elul 5369/1609, at the age of ninety-seven, the Maharal's long and productive life came to an end. Eight months later, his faithful wife, Perl, also passed away and was buried next to him in the Prague cemetery. A large double headstone was erected with the simple inscription, "Rabbi Yehudah son of Rabbi Betzalel and his wife that he chose, Perl daughter of Shmuel." At some later date a lengthy inscription extolling the great achievements of the Maharal and his wife was engraved all around the sides and top of the graves.

His Legacy

Our Sages said that *tzaddikim* are considered alive even after they die. The Maharal's spiritual legacy has forever enriched the Jewish people, and his voice still speaks to us through his writings and his innovative ideas.

Although his complete educational reform never took hold, some parts of his program became incorporated into the accepted framework of Torah education. Most notable is the study of the Mishnah. In our day, when the importance of studying Mishnah is taken for granted, we sometimes forget that we have to be grateful to the Maharal and his student, the *Tosafos Yom Tov*, for this.

But by far the greatest gift the Maharal endowed on his people is his approach to understanding the aggadic teachings of the Sages. The Maharal taught that every statement of the Sages contains a message. Whether the facts recorded actually happened or are to be understood in a metaphoric or allegorical way is secondary to their main purpose, which is to teach the wisdom of Torah.

Countless statements of the *aggadah* that seem at first to be incomprehensible or pointless take on a profound meaning when viewed through the illuminating lens of the Maharal's analysis.

Once the Maharal's method of interpretation has been assimilated by the student into his own mental-process, he will find that it can be used to plumb the depths of many other sayings of the Sages which the Maharal did not directly relate to.

It has been said that if we apply the Maharal's approach to the legend of the *golem* he is purported to have created out of clay, we will find that the hidden message is that the Maharal took the *aggados* of our Sages that had lain hitherto as a lifeless clump of clay for lack of appreciation and breathed into them life, transforming them into powerful tools to ward off attacks from alien quarters.

The Maharal Today

In truth, despite the wide acclaim and wide esteem in which the Maharal was held even during his lifetime, his writings lay unappreciated for at least one hundred and fifty years. The first to apply themselves to his teachings were the third generation proponents of the Chasidic movement in the eighteenth century.

The founder of Chabad *chasidus*, Rabbi Shneur Zalman of Liadi, himself a descendant of the Maharal, incorporated some of his ideas into his *sefer*, the *Tanya*. Rabbi Yisrael Hopstein, the *Maggid* of Koznitz, attached great importance to the works of the Maharal and was instrumental in having them reprinted. The current editions of the Maharal's works contain a number of pieces the *Maggid* wrote to clarify some difficulties in the Maharal.

But it was among the followers of Rabbi Bunim of Parshischa and his successor, Rabbi Mendel of Kotzk, that the Maharal's works were given most prominence. They advocated studying the Maharal's works as a substitute for the *Zohar*, whose esoteric ideas are often difficult to fathom. The writings of the *Shem MiShmuel* of Sochatchov and the *Sefas Emes* of Gur, both offshoots of Kotzk, are heavily influenced by the Maharal's teachings.

The world of *Mussar* was also influenced by the Maharal. The major disciple of Rabbi Yisrael Salanter, Rabbi Simchah Zissel Ziv of Kelm, based many of his ideas on the Maharal. More recently, in our generation, Rabbi Eliyahu Eliezer Dessler taught his students how to understand the Maharal's insights in terms that could be applied to their own personal growth. The most popular British edition of the complete works of the Maharal is a direct result of the interest that Rabbi Dessler engendered among his students in the rich legacy of the Maharal. This edition included also the first edition of the Maharal's commentary on the *aggados* that had lain unpublished for three hundred and fifty years.

Another great propagator of the Maharal's thought in recent times was Rabbi Yitzchak Hutner, whose work *Pachad Yitzchak* draws heavily on the Maharal.

Conclusion

In his lifetime, the Maharal was acclaimed and respected as a powerful Torah leader and a major halachic authority. Among the common folk, he was revered as a legendary figure around whom various fantastic legends grew. Most of these appear to be the product of fertile imaginative minds, with very little historical basis but they nevertheless serve to demonstrate the unique regard in which he was held.

But his major contribution to Torah thought took over three hundred years to gain full appreciation. It is in our post-Holocaust generation, which is preparing itself physically and spiritually to greet the Mashiach, that the Maharal's teachings are quoted most often. The positiveness and optimism that permeates all his writing strikes a responsive chord in the hearts of so many Jews seeking meaning and depth in a shallow world. The insight and perception that his ideas develop in our minds are a further step in preparing us for the final days when "the earth shall be full of the knowledge of Hashem like the waters that cover the sea" (*Yeshayahu* 11:9).

NOTE: This introduction is based mainly on the well-researched article of Dr. A. Gottsdiner, included in the standard editions of the Maharal's writings. Yaakov Dovid Shulman's novel, *The Maharal of Prague*, was also helpful.

Maharal
EMERGING PATTERNS

1
Avraham

ONE OF THE BASIC tenets of Judaism is that everything in the world exists only because God wills it to exist, and that every event that occurs does so because God wills it to occur. Another fundamental fact is that the Torah is the book in which God reveals His will to the Jewish People — who in turn are entrusted to transmit His will to the nations of the world.

Ma'asei Avos Siman Labanim

Since the phenomena and occurrences in the world express God's will, and the Torah expresses God's will, then the world and the Torah are intrinsically connected. Each and every detail of all that exists, as well as each and every detail of all that has ever occurred, must be contained somewhere in the Torah.[1]

The Talmud (*Sotah* 34a) alludes to this in the words *ma'asei avos siman labanim* — "The lives of the fathers [patriarchs] are a prototype of the destiny of the sons [the Jewish People]."

Not only does all of world history lie encoded within the words of the Torah, but even more specifically, the history of the Jewish People is encapsulated in the lives of its three patriarchs, Avraham, Yitzchak, and Yaakov.

In very general terms, the Jews have experienced three eras in

---

1. The Midrash (*Bereshis Rabbah* 1:1) says: "God looked into the Torah and [then] created the world." God looked into the Torah, the blueprint of creation, and then used that "master plan" to create the world.

their national history:

1. The Egypt and Sinai Desert Experience.
   The Jews began their history as slaves in Egypt, where they suffered bitterly for many years. They were finally redeemed by God and brought to Mount Sinai, where they received the Divine Torah. Then, they spent forty relatively peaceful years in the desert, during which time they incorporated the lessons they learned at Sinai into their national consciousness.[2]
2. The *Mishkan* and the Temple Era.
   After crossing the Jordan River and settling in the Land of Israel, the Jews, for the most part, enjoyed a vibrant and thriving life, governed by the laws of the Torah. This continued for hundreds of years, until the destruction of the First Temple. After a seventy-year exile in Babylonia, they built a Second Temple and again enjoyed a spiritual life. Although this period was not nearly as great as the period of the First Temple, the Jews were still able to offer *korbanos* in the Second Temple and live on their own land. This era came to a close at the end of the Second Temple period, when anarchy set in and civil war broke out. It was then that the Romans succeeded in destroying the Temple.
3. The Diaspora Experience.
   With the destruction of the Second Temple, the Jews were dispersed and exiled to countries in many different parts of the world. For nearly two thousand years they have survived as a people estranged from its land, lacking a Temple and the governance of Torah.

---

2. The number forty is very significant. It is related to the concept of the realization of a new beginning. The basic form of a fetus is completed after forty days (*Niddah* 30a); the flood in Noach's day rained water for forty days and nights (*Bereshis* 7:17), to make way for a new civilization; and the Jews stayed in the desert for forty years to prepare themselves for a new beginning in the Land of Israel.

These three experiences are mirrored in the lives of our patriarchs.
1. Avraham, our first patriarch, endured much suffering in his early years. At the mere age of three he began his spiritual odyssey, leading to his discovery of One God and the dissemination of this concept to others. As a result, he was persecuted not only by society, but even by his own family. Nimrod, the ruler of Avraham's land, sought to kill him for his beliefs by throwing him into a flaming furnace.

   It was only when Avraham was seventy-five years old that God told him he would father a great nation (*Bereshis* 12:2). But from that point on, his life would be (relatively) peaceful. He lived in the Land of Israel, was blessed with fame and wealth, and merited to see his son Yitzchak continue his spiritual mission.

   In this way, Avraham's life paralleled the first experience of our people: It began with difficulty (Avraham's troubles in Ur Kasdim, and the Jewish People's enslavement in Egypt), but ended in tranquillity (Avraham's life in the Land of Israel, seeing his son continue in his path, and the desert years for the Jews, receiving the Torah and seeing it carried on by their sons).
2. Yitzchak, the second patriarch, began his life in physical and spiritual abundance. He grew up in the spiritual aura of Avraham's household and spent his entire life in the Land of Israel; he was also fabulously wealthy. The end of his life, however, was difficult. He suffered not only from blindness, but also from the knowledge that his two sons had chosen divergent paths in life, with one (Esav) bent on destroying his brother (Yaakov). Yitzchak's life, in that sense, paralleled our second national experience, which began in the ideal state of living in our own land in the aura of the Holy Temple, but ended in anarchy.
3. Our third patriarch, Yaakov, lived a life beset by troubles. As a young man, he was forced to flee his brother Esav who

sought to kill him. When he took refuge with his Uncle Lavan, he was manipulated into working for him for fourteen years. When he finally decided to leave, Lavan tried to swindle him out of his pay. After returning to the Land of Israel, he was met by Esav, who still wanted to kill him. His daughter Dinah was violated by a neighboring prince, and two of his sons put him in mortal danger by massacring the entire city of Shechem. His son Yosef was taken from him and presumed dead for twenty-two years. Eventually, Yaakov was forced to resettle in Egypt, a morally corrupt land, where he lived out his remaining years.

This is analogous to our third national experience, in the diaspora, which has been filled with troubles: fleeing from danger, being mistreated by others for no reason, and being forced to resettle in new, difficult lands.

* * *

The Torah's description of the lives of our patriarchs thus spells out Jewish destiny: *ma'asei avos siman labanim*.

Yet there is one more bit of information that relates to our sequence. The Talmud (*Ta'anis* 5b) says: "Our patriarch Yaakov never died…. Just as his descendants live on, so too he lives on." This is the final message to the Jewish People. True, Jewish history in the diaspora will be a story of one struggle after another, but, nonetheless, the Jewish People will reach a time when "they will live forever." The long diaspora will give way to an era when the Jews will live without troubles and without suffering, and will experience only pure spiritual bliss.[3]

Avraham and Jewish History

There is a very specific connection between the life of Avraham and the experience of the Jewish People in Egypt.

Avraham was born in the city of Ur Kasdim, an extremely im-

---

3. Maharal, *Derech Chaim* 5:4.

moral place.

The Talmud[4] says: "God regretted creating the people of Ur Kasdim because they were so bad, as it is written, 'The land of Kasdim, it does not deserve to exist.'"[5] The Midrash adds that the only reason that Ur Kasdim did exist was in Avraham's merit.

The Midrash[6] also says (commenting on *Bereshis* 2:4, "These are the things that developed from the heavens and the earth, when they were created," בהבראם): בהבראם has the letters א-ב-ר-ה-ם (Avraham) in it. The message implied is that the *entire world* was worthy of being created on Avraham's behalf. Not only did Ur Kasdim stand on Avraham's merit, but all of creation existed on his merit alone.

The Talmud[7] says: "This world will exist for six thousand years. The first two thousand years are 'the two thousand years of nothingness,' the second two thousand years are 'the two thousand years of Torah,' and the third two millennia are 'the two thousand years of the messianic era.'"

The "two thousand years of Torah," the Talmud adds, commenced when Avraham began teaching Torah to the people around him. (Avraham was born in the year 1948 from creation, and began teaching people Torah at the age of fifty-two.)

Avraham initiated a new era in world history: He introduced humanity to a new relationship with God. He was the quintessential beginner.

By definition, a beginner is someone who is not connected to his surroundings. He breaks out of the existing social structure. The more dissimilar he is from those around him, the more of an innovator he is. Avraham, as a consummate beginner, was at the polar opposite of the society which surrounded him. The people of Ur Kasdim were not worthy even of existing, and Avraham

---

4. *Sukkah* 52b.
5. *Yeshayahu* 23:13; Rashi ad. loc.
6. *Bereshis Rabbah* 12:9.
7. *Sanhedrin* 97a.

was worthy of the *entire world* being created in his merit.[8]

* * *

How does Avraham's experience connect to the Jewish People's experience in Egypt?

The Jews were enslaved in Egypt, a land steeped in profound moral corruption; Jewish national history began in a land whose people held antithetical values to their own. The Jews' experience therefore mirrors Avraham's, but on a national level: What Avraham was as an individual vis-à-vis his surroundings, the Jewish People were as a nation vis-à-vis theirs. The Jews were the expansion of Avraham into a people; a people who would bring monotheism and spirituality to humanity. The Jews were beginners, too.

That is why the Jewish People began their history in a land that was antithetical to all they stood for: An innovator is only an innovator if he is fundamentally different from his surroundings.[9]

---

8. The "beginning factor" in Avraham's life is spoken of in the Torah in another way, too. Just before God tells Avraham "*Lech Lecha*/Go from your land, from your birthplace and from your father's house [to found the Jewish People]" (*Bereshis* 12:1), the Torah tells of the death of Avraham's father, Terach (*Bereshis* 11:32). In reality, Terach died many years later.

While it is common for the death of an older person to be mentioned before the life story of a younger person, even if he is still alive (e.g. Noach's death is mentioned before Avraham's birth, even though he died fifty-eight years later), it is only done in the context of chronicling. (See, for example, *Bereshis* 25:8, where Avraham's death is followed by "And these are the descendants of Yitzchak"; Avraham was alive at the time [*Bereshis* 25:19].)

In this case, the death of Terach is mentioned before "Go from your land...," which is *not* a chronicle of Avraham. (If it were it would have said "And these are the descendants of Avraham...")

The message of the juxtaposition is this: Avraham was totally different from his surroundings. When he left his surroundings to serve God, he no longer had any connection to them — even to his family. It was as if his biological father had died.

9. Maharal, *Gevuros Hashem*, chapter 5.

Avraham Kept All of Torah

The Midrash[10] tells us that Avraham, Yitzchak, and Yaakov lived their lives in accordance with the Torah, which would not be given until many centuries later at Sinai.

Interestingly, our tradition also teaches that Avraham kept the entire Torah (*Yoma* 28b), Yitzchak kept the laws of *shechitah* (*Bereshis* 27:30; see Rashi ad. loc.), and Yaakov kept the laws of Shabbos (see *Shabbos* 118b).

Why is only Avraham mentioned as having kept all of Torah, if the other patriarchs did too?

Consider this thought: Avraham's defining *middah* (character trait) was *chesed*, doing good to others; he spent his lifetime bringing people close to God through acts of loving-kindness and hospitality. The Torah, too, can be seen as essentially an instrument of *chesed*. Its goal is to guide man to reach the ultimate good, the ultimate pleasure in this world, which is knowing God. In fact, the Torah is called *Toras Chesed* for that reason.[11] Thus, Avraham's defining *middah* parallels a major aspect of Torah. The other patriarchs, although they too observed the entire Torah, did not share this *chesed*-based connection to Torah, and therefore are not specifically mentioned as having kept all of the Torah.

The Talmud (*Kiddushin* 31a) says that one who is commanded to perform a mitzvah merits a greater reward for keeping it than

---

There is a source for the parallel of Avraham and the Jewish People in the Torah, too. In *Bereshis* 15:7, God says to Avraham: "I am God *Who took [Avraham] out of* Ur Kasdim." In *Shemos* 20:2, God uses similar language in referring to the Jewish People: "I am the Lord your God *Who took [the Jews] out of* the land of Egypt."

10. *Pesikta Zutresa; Mikeitz* 43:16.

11. See *Mishlei* 31:26 and *Sukkah* 49b. See also *Sotah* 14a, where Rabbi Simla'i says: *"The Torah begins with chesed (God's clothing Adam and Chavah) and ends with chesed (God's burying Moshe)."* This implies that the essence of Torah is *chesed*, to encourage man to perform deeds of kindness and to reward him for doing so.

one who is not commanded to keep it.

Avraham's observance of Torah was of greater significance than the other patriarchs' because only he was "commanded" by his very nature to keep it. That is why only he is mentioned as having kept all of Torah.[12]

Why Avraham Was Given the Mitzvah of *Milah*

Avraham's uniqueness is demonstrated by the fact that the mitzvah of circumcision (*milah*) was given to Avraham long before the rest of Torah was given to the Jewish People at Mount Sinai.

Avraham, as an individual, was unable to formally receive the entire Torah, as Torah could only be given to a whole nation.[13] Why, then, was the mitzvah of circumcision singled out to be given to him?

Avraham lived in a pagan society that was completely rooted in the physical world and spiritually primitive. People believed in multiple gods who were not Divine, but finite and limited beings, albeit much greater and more powerful than human beings. These arbitrary "deities" could be "appeased" from their wrath with sacrifices and could also be "fooled" if necessary.

In effect, then, humanity in Avraham's time lacked any connection with the Omniscient Creator of the world. People were so totally divorced from an understanding of God that it was as if a dense, impenetrable barrier separated Him from them.[14]

Avraham was the first human being to recognize a Unified, Infinite Creator, and to promulgate His existence amongst his fellow men. Avraham, in essence, removed the barrier separating man from God, and connected man to Him.

---

12. Maharal, *Tiferes Yisrael*, chapter 20.
13. See chapter 8.
14. Man, in essence, projected his own image onto his gods. He created gods which were huge, but who had the same flaws as man (i.e. anger, jealousy, selfishness, etc.).

Milah accomplishes the same thing. The act of circumcision removes the foreskin — a physical covering that, metaphysically, serves to separate man from God. Since the mitzvah of *milah* is analogous to the primary accomplishment of Avraham's life, it is therefore fitting that Avraham received it even before the revelation of the entire Torah at Sinai.[15]

Avraham and the Four Kings

The Torah recounts the story of the Four Kings battling the Five Kings, vanquishing them, and capturing Avraham's nephew, Lot, from the city of Sodom. It tells us that Avraham sought to free Lot and was forced to fight the Four Kings to do so; he roundly defeated them. The Midrash says that the only reason the Four Kings captured Lot was in order to draw Avraham into the war, as they hoped to kill him. What is the deeper meaning of the Four Kings' struggle against the Five Kings, and why did they seek to destroy Avraham?

In the Torah, every number has a philosophical significance; each number represents a different concept.[16] The number one, for example, represents Godliness, Oneness, and Unity.[17]

The number four represents physicality; the physical world extends in four directions (north, south, east, and west). Four is the antithesis of the number one, which symbolizes Godliness and spirituality. Symbolically, then, the number four represents the four directions from which one can leave, or "depart" the Unity of God.

Let us now study the number five. The number five has the very same properties as the number four — indicating physicality — but with an additional "one," or an inner, central point, which unites the four sides; hence, physicality which has a spiri-

---

15. *Tiferes Yisrael*, chapter 19.
16. See chapters 7 and 9 for more lengthy discussions on the matter.
17. Truth is also represented by the number one, as there is one truth, but many falsehoods.

tual component.

The Four Kings represented a people who were the epitome of the physical.

The Five Kings represented a people who had a physical "four" side to them, but who also had a "one" aspect of spiritual-

ity. It was their "one-side," their higher spiritual awareness, that the Four Kings abhorred and wanted to destroy. That is why they fought them. After they destroyed the Five Kings and were emboldened by their victory, the Four Kings captured Lot. They hoped to draw Avraham, the consummate human "one," or spiritual being — their nemesis — into the war, to destroy him.

Avraham, throughout his life, set the pattern that our whole people would be destined to follow in the two thousand years of Torah.

2
Bris Bein Habesarim

Genesis: Chapter 15

AFTER THESE EVENTS, the word of God was [addressed] to Avram in a vision, saying, *"Avram, do not be afraid! I will act as a protection for you, [and] your reward will be very great."*

Avram responded, *"My Lord, God! What is [the benefit of] what You will give me [if] I am going to be obliterated..."*

Just then, the word of God was [addressed] to him, saying, *"...he who will be produced by your body will inherit from you."* God took him outside and said [to him], *"Look now towards the heavens and count the stars... So will be your descendants."* He believed God, and [God] considered this for him as an act of righteousness.

He then said to him, *"I am God Who took you out of Ur Kasdim to give you this land, to take possession of it."*

[Avram] said, *"My Lord, God! How will I know that I shall take possession of it?"*

[God] then said to him, *"Bring [before] Me three calves, three goats, three rams, a turtledove and a young [common dove]."* He brought all these [before] Him, split them down the middle...but the birds he did not split....

As the sun was setting, a deep sleep came over Avram...

[God] said to Avram, *"You shall surely know that your descendants will be foreigners in a land that is not theirs, and [the inhabitants] will enslave them and oppress them for four hundred years. And I will also carry out judgment on the nation that enslaves [them], and after that they will leave with great wealth.... The fourth generation will return here....*" On that day, God formed a covenant with Avram, saying, "*I have given your descendants this land — from the river of Mitzrayim until the great river, the River Peras...*"

"After These Events"

In the above-mentioned covenant, called the *Bris Bein Habesarim* (Covenant between the Parts), God details to Avraham[1] the destiny of his progeny: They will be enslaved for four hundred years in a foreign land, after which time God will redeem them and bring them into the Land of Israel, to be His chosen people.

The *Bris Bein Habesarim* begins with the words, "*After these events, the word of God was [addressed] to Avram...*"

To which "events" is the Torah referring?

The Midrash (*Bereshis Rabbah* 44:5) explains that at this point in time Avraham felt uncertain as to whether he still merited to father the Jewish People. It was after certain events had taken place[2] that God came to assure Avraham that he would indeed be the progenitor of the Jews.

The Midrash[3] elaborates:

> Why was Avraham fearful? R. Levi says: Avraham had been successful in his war against the Four Kings. He now feared that the other nations would gather and wage war against him in revenge.
>
> Also, he worried that he had killed innocent people in his war against the Four Kings, and that this would cause him to lose his merit to father the Jewish People.
>
> The Rabbis say: Avraham was concerned that because

---

1. For the sake of fluency, the discussion in this chapter will use the name "Avraham," even though, at this point in time, our patriarch's name was still "Avram."
2. God had already told Avraham in *Bereshis* 12:2 that he would be made into a great, Godly people.
3. *Midrash Rabbah* 44:4 (paraphrased).

so many miracles had happened to him — including his successful war against the Four Kings — he may have used up his merits, and would no longer have the merit to father the Jewish People.

God's response to Avraham's concern is enumerated a few verses later: "Avram, do not be afraid! I will act as a protection for you, [and] your reward will be very great."

How did God's response address Avraham's fear?

According to R. Levi's understanding of Avraham's fear (being attacked by other nations), God was telling him: "Do not be afraid; I will act as a protection for you against the nations."

Regarding his worries that he had killed innocent people, God was saying: "Your reward will be very great; nothing that you have done will detract from your future reward."

According to the Rabbis, however, the second half of the verse means something else: "Your reward will be great: You still have a great reward awaiting you. The miracles that have occurred on your behalf have not used up your merits, and you will yet merit to father the Jewish People."[4]

Avraham's Fear

In *Bereshis* 12:2, God promises Avraham that he will be the forefather of the Jewish People: "I will make you into a great nation."

Yet, in *Bereshis* 15:2, Avraham expresses doubt that this will happen: "What is [the benefit of] what You will give me [when I do not have a child]," he asks.

Why was Avraham unsure? Hadn't God promised him that he would father a great nation?

Consider: There are two ways in which God can make a promise to a human being: (a) with a prophecy (or *nevuah*); (b)

---

4. *Gevuros Hashem*, chapter 6.
   It is apparent in the above Midrash (as interpreted by the Rabbis) that it is possible to use up one's merits in this world. The addendum to this chapter contains a more extensive discussion on the subject.

with an assurance (or *havtachah*).

A *prophecy* predicts something that will definitely happen, regardless of the recipient's future actions or merits.

An *assurance* predicts something that may or may not happen, depending on the worthiness of the recipient at the time that the event should take place.

Thus, prophecy cannot change,[5] but an assurance can, as a person can lose his merits.[6]

In fact, we find that prophecies and assurances are recorded differently in the Torah.

Prophecies are always recorded in the past tense[7]: It is as if the events have already occurred, since it is God Himself Who predicts them. Assurances are spoken of in the future tense, as they depend on the future merits of the recipient.

That is why Avraham was fearful: God's promise to him that he would have children had been in the form of an assurance (it was said in the future tense), and not as a prophecy (in the past tense).

After his victory against the Four Kings (for a reason disputed by R. Levi and the Rabbis) he feared that he no longer held the

---

5. That is, a good prophecy. The Prophet Yonah prophesied that the city of Ninveh would be destroyed, yet the people repented and were spared (*Yonah* 3:4).

The explanation is that prophecies, as a rule, cannot be changed. However, as God's essence is good, a prophecy that is bad is more connected to the recipient than it is to God. Since a person can always change, God allows bad prophecies to be changed for good. Accordingly, Daniel's prophecy of the destruction of Nevuchadnetzar was a good one (for the Jews) and could not be changed.

6. A prophet whose prophecies do not come true is a false prophet, and must be put to death (*Devarim* 18:20). This is only true regarding prophecies of good tidings that do not come true.

7. For example, God told the Prophet Chananya ben Azur: "Behold I *have broken* the yoke of [Nevuchadnetzar] the king of Babylonia" (*Yirmeyahu* 28:2), even though that event had not yet occurred.

merits to become the father of the Jewish People.[8]

"Go Outside" and Avraham's Doubt

In the *Bris Bein Habesarim*, God takes Avraham outside and says to him: "Look now towards the heavens and count the stars, if it is possible for you to count them.... So will be your descendants."

What is the deeper meaning of this episode?

The Talmud[9] explains that originally, Avraham was destined to be childless. When God "took him outside," it was as if He was saying to him, "Go out" and transcend your old destiny and its limitations. You now have a new destiny, one that harbors new potential. You will indeed bear children, and those children will multiply and grow into an entire nation.

Perhaps Avraham's fear of not having children is related to this point. Perhaps he knew that having children would require a fundamental change in his destiny — and that would require a miracle.

Let us examine the concept of "change" as it relates to this topic.

The physical world is comprised of four increasingly complex levels of existence: inanimate, plant, animal, and human. The less complex an entity is, the easier it is for it to change. A rock, for example, which is on the lowest level of creation, can be changed relatively easily (by breaking or sculpting). It is much more difficult to change a plant, and even more difficult to change an animal's physical makeup (through genetic engineering). But even

---

8. *Gevuros Hashem*, chapter 7.

In *Bereshis* 32:11–12, Yaakov prays to God: "I have become unworthy through all the acts of kindness... that You carried out for Your servant.... Please save me from the hand of my brother, from the hand of Esav." Yaakov worried because he had only been *assured* that he would return to his father's home in peace (*Bereshis* 28:15). He was thus afraid that he had sinned in the interim and had lost his merit to protection (see *Berachos* 4a).

9. *Shabbos* 156a (not a direct translation).

an animal's physical makeup can be changed more easily than can a human being's.

The level of complexity of even the most intricate physical entity, however, is still less complex than the most basic *meta*-physical object. This is apparent from the fact that while all physical entities can be defined in concrete terms, a metaphysical entity (such as an angel) cannot.

That is why Avraham was fearful: He knew that his destiny did not include having children. A person's destiny is metaphysical by nature, and thus a great miracle would be required to change it, allowing him to have children. Avraham feared that any small wrongdoing he may have done would have eliminated the merit he would need for this to occur. He therefore feared that his destiny would remain unchanged.[10]

Your Children Will Be Enslaved for Four Hundred Years

In the *Bris Bein Habesarim*, God tells Avraham that his children will endure a period of slavery in a foreign land. The number four appears twice in the prophecy: The slavery will last four hundred years, and the fourth generation to be enslaved will be freed.

What is the significance of the number four? And why does it recur here?

As mentioned in chapter one, the number four represents the four directions from which one can leave the "One," Godly point. Four thus symbolizes the concept of departure from that which is True.

The nature of the Jews is to be a free and noble people.[11] Slavery was a departure from our natural state of being, much as the number four is a departure from the "One" original point. Our slavery, in a deeper way, embodied the concept of "four," and its duration was expressed as a multiple of four.

---

10. *Gevuros Hashem*, chapter 7.

11. As it says, "And you will be a kingdom of nobles and a holy nation for Me" (*Shemos* 19:6).

That is also why our slavery in Egypt was limited to four generations. After we had experienced slavery in the full dimension of "four," we had already left our central "One-point" in every possible direction. We simply could not be enslaved anymore.[12]

Interestingly, our people will also experience four exiles before the ultimate redemption arrives: (1) Babylonia; (2) Persia; (3) Greece; and (4) Rome (the exile we are presently in, after which time we will return to the Land of Israel).

Childlessness and Inheriting the Land of Israel

The *Bris Bein Habesarim* opens with God's telling Avraham that he will have children. He assures him: "He who will be produced by your body will inherit from you." Avraham trusts God's assurance, as it says: "[Avraham] believed God, and [God] considered this for him as an act of righteousness." Yet, a few verses later, when God tells Avraham that he will receive the Land of Israel,[13] Avraham questions God: "How will I know that I shall take possession of it?"

There are two ways to understand Avraham's doubts about receiving the land, and not about having children:

1. Avraham was confident that he would have children, and was also confident that he would inherit the Land of Israel. His concern was that his progeny would not be able to *maintain* their existence in it. He knew that they were bound to sin in future times, and would thereupon be expelled from the land. His concern was, "How will I know that they shall take possession of it *eternally*? With what merit, then, will my children be allowed to *return* to the Land of Israel after they sin?"

2. While Avraham was confident that he would have children, he worried that his progeny would not have the

---

12. *Gevuros Hashem*, chapter 10.
13. "I am God, Who took you out of Ur Kasdim to give you this land, to take possession of it" (*Bereshis* 15:7).

merit to inherit the Land of Israel because of its immense spirituality. "With what merit will the Jewish People inherit the Land of Israel, *the most sublime land on Earth*," he asked.[14]

Ownership means "bringing an entity into your possession." The things a person owns are connected to him — and one can only connect to things on the same spiritual level as he is. Thus, Avraham feared that his children would not reach the spiritual level necessary to connect to, and deserve to "possess," the spiritual and holy Land of Israel.

* * *

God's reply to Avraham was this: "Bring [before] Me three calves, three goats, three rams, a turtledove and a young [common dove]." The Midrash (*Bereshis Rabbah* 44:14) teaches us that God was telling Avraham that his children would inherit the Land of Israel in the merit of the *korbanos*. Avraham brought ten offerings, each of which represented a *korban* that the Jews would bring in the Temple.[15]

Let us try to understand God's reply to Avraham in this context.

According to the first explanation of Avraham's fear (eternal possession), we can understand God's reply in the following

---

14. The Land of Israel is different from any other land on Earth, because the land itself is holy. This holiness expresses itself in many ways. For example, the Omer (made of wheat, brought on Passover), *Bikkurim* (first fruits), and *Shtei Halechem* (two breads, brought on Shavuos) offerings each requires a level of holiness such that they may only be brought from produce grown in Israel (*Keilim* 1:6).

15. The Midrash (*Midrash Rabbah* 44:17) explains that the three calves corresponded to the "calf of Yom Kippur," the "calf of all mitzvos," and the *"eiglah arufah."* The three goats corresponded to the "goat of the festivals," the "goat of *Rosh Chodesh*," and the "goat of an individual." The three rams corresponded to the *"asham vadai,"* the *"asham talui"* (both of which were rams), and the "sheep of an individual."

way: A person who is usually clean and then gets dirty, can clean himself easily with a simple bath. A person who works in the mud and is continually dirty, however, will not be able to clean himself completely even with a thorough bath.

Korbanos, which bring a person atonement for unintentional sins, are a great gift from God. When accompanied by sincere remorse, they are a relatively easy means of atonement. The fact that this simple atonement is effective for the Jewish People implies that the Jews are generally "clean," or on a high spiritual plane.

God told Avraham that the Jews will receive the Land of Israel eternally because they have korbanos. The fact that the Jews can always "clean" themselves with a simple washing, i.e. with korbanos and repentance, implies that they will be allowed back into the Land of Israel as soon as they repent.[16]

According to the second explanation of Avraham's fear (his children would not be worthy of the Land of Israel's holiness), God's reply was: Your children will inherit the spiritual Land of Israel in the merit of the offerings they will bring: The fact that your descendants will have the ability to come close to Me through korbanos, as no one else can, implies that they will have a nature that is entirely unique. There will be a component in their soul that is very close to God. That is why they will receive the Land of Israel, a land of sublime spirituality.[17]

Three Calves, Three Goats, Three Rams, and a Bird

God told Avraham to offer three calves, three goats, three rams,

---

16. A slightly different approach: The word קרבן comes from the root "קרב," or *closeness*. God was telling Avraham that the fact that the Jews have korbanos, and are able to come close to God, gives them a special connection to eternity. Thus, while no other nation can receive a land "eternally," the Jewish People are able to receive the Land of Israel eternally (*Gevuros Hashem*, chapter 8).

17. *Gevuros Hashem*, chapter 8.

and one bird. As mentioned above, these each represented a category of offerings that would be brought in the Temple.

What is the deeper meaning of the sequence of three times three plus one, which brings the sum to ten?

In the physical world, every object is composed of three potential parts: a beginning, a middle, and an end. Every object has these three parts in both its length and its width. Thus, in a deeper way, every physical object has within itself the potential for nine parts.[18]

	Beginning	Middle	End
Beginning			
Middle			
End			

In fact, the deeper meaning of the number nine is "all the separate parts that exist in a physical entity."

The deeper meaning of the number ten is the step after nine. It represents not the separate parts of an entity, but the unity that all nine parts achieve when they merge and are united as one.

Avraham offered a total of ten *korbanos*. The nine animals represented all of the individual offerings that the Jews would bring in the Temple. The tenth *korban*, the bird, represented the total concept of *korbanos* — the unifying factor in the disparate nine.

Thus, the first nine offerings were broken in half — an action

---

18. Maharal does not count the three potential parts that exist in the depth of every item (which would bring the total to twenty-seven parts), perhaps because although all items have an *apparent* length and width, not all items appear to have depth.

analogous to sacrificing *korbanos* on the altar of later times[19] — but the bird was not broken. The bird did not represent an offering, but the *entire concept* of offerings, and thus there was no reason for it to be broken.[20]

Addendum:
Reward in This World vs. Reward in the Next World

The Midrash mentioned earlier in this chapter, and explained in footnote 4, implies that one can lose his reward in the next world by receiving benefit in this world.

Mishnah *Pe'ah* 1:1 discusses this topic: *"These are the things for which one reaps reward in this world, yet retains the principal reward for the world to come*:

1. *Honoring one's father and mother;*
2. *Doing chesed for one's fellow;*
3. *Bringing peace between two people."*

One would expect that good deeds would be rewarded only in the next world. Yet we are told that these three mitzvos are exceptions and bring reward in this world, too. Are these three mitzvos more significant than others? Why are they the only ones for which we receive reward in this world?

Perhaps these three mitzvos mentioned are not individual mitzvos, but rather categories that together encapsulate the entire range of the interpersonal mitzvos (*bein adam lechaveiro*).

The first mitzvah mentioned is honoring parents. As children, we see our parents as great, wise, strong, and infallible. As we get older, we begin to see their limitations, but they are still powerful

---

19. *Gevuros Hashem*, chapter 5. See also Ramban on *Bereshis* 15:10.
20. *Gevuros Hashem*, chapter 8.

The number ten is represented by the letter "י." It is the most unified letter in the Hebrew alphabet; compared to the other "structured" letters, it is a simple dot. Moreover, the letter י has no connection to the "floor" of the parchment line; it is as if it is "flying," similar to the bird which was the tenth offering.

forces in our lives and we revere them. Our parents thus represent the "higher level" of society.

The second mitzvah mentioned is doing kindness for people in need. Society generally sees needy people as the "lower class," since they are dependent on others for their needs.

The third mitzvah mentioned is making peace between two people who are having a dispute. Usually, people who fight with each other are from the same socio-economic level. At the root of most disputes lies the fact that one person feels threatened by the success his fellow. In contrast, a poor person is not intimidated by the success of a wealthy person (it is totally out of his realm), and a wealthy person is not threatened by the success of a poor person. Thus, one who brings peace between warring parties is acting kindly to people of equal social levels, whether they be rich, poor, or of moderate means.

These three mitzvos, then, represent the entire spectrum of positive interpersonal relations: The first two represent the extremes, and the third represents the entire continuum. The Mishnah is saying that the performance of *all* interpersonal mitzvos merits reward in this world and the next.

Another way to understand how these mitzvos comprise the entire continuum is this:

There are three types of interpersonal mitzvos: intuitive, non-intuitive, and those that fall somewhere in between.

Honoring parents is something that logic obligates us to do. We are duty-bound to respect and revere them out of gratitude for all they have done for us.

Supporting poor people is something our logic would not necessarily tell us to do. Why should we be obligated to give another person what we worked hard to attain?

Bringing peace between two disputing parties is something that falls between these two extremes. It is not really intuitive, yet neither is it illogical. On one hand we shouldn't be obligated to get involved in other people's disputes, but on the other hand, we know that God despises senseless hatred between people, and this knowledge should motivate us to try to bring peace between the two parties.

The Mishnah uses these three examples to tell us that *all* interpersonal mitzvos reap reward in this world: those that are mandated by logic, those that are not mandated by logic, and those that fall somewhere in between.[21]

Why Interpersonal Mitzvos Reap Reward in This World

Why should the performance of interpersonal mitzvos bring one reward in this world?

Consider this thought: The essence of God is *chesed*. God needs nothing from anybody and is the Ultimate Giver.

One who does good to his fellow human being by fulfilling the positive interpersonal commandments is emulating God. Judaism teaches that when one emulates God he taps into His essence.

Since the very essence of God is goodness, it follows that the more a person taps into it, the more goodness he will receive.

Thus, even though the reward for mitzvos is supposed to be in the next world, one who does good to his fellow cannot help but receive good from God in this world too.[22]

---

21. *Gevuros Hashem*, chapter 6.
22. This thought expands on Maharal's words.

3
Yosef

THE TORAH TELLS US in great detail how Yosef, more than any other person, served as the catalyst that brought Avraham's descendants to Egypt to live out the enslavement God had promised Avraham at the *Bris Bein Habesarim*. The events that brought Yosef to a position from which he could effect the family's descent to Egypt were numerous and complex.

Yosef has recurrent dreams of royalty, which arouse his brothers' animosity and fear. They sell him into slavery in Egypt. Soon after, he is arrested on contrived charges and thrown into a dungeon. Ten years later, he meets the imprisoned royal butler, who, two years later, has Yosef brought before Pharaoh to interpret his dream. Pharaoh is impressed with Yosef's wisdom and makes him viceroy of Egypt. From that position he is able to bring the family down to Egypt.

Why was it necessary for Yosef to be sold as a slave, thrown into a dungeon for a full twelve years, and only *then* be raised to the level of viceroy, to be able to bring his family down to Egypt? Why not have Yosef go down to Egypt to buy food, meet an advisor of Pharaoh who is impressed with his wisdom and arranges a meeting with Pharaoh, who then appoints him to the position of viceroy?

The Consummate Tzurah

There is clearly something about Yosef's character that made it essential for him to first be enslaved and then incarcerated in a dungeon for an extended period of time, before he could rise to a position of leadership.

In order to understand Yosef's character, it is necessary to first explain two important concepts: *chomer* and *tzurah*.

There are two aspects to everything that exists in the world. One is the *chomer*, or the raw material of which things are made, and the other is the *tzurah*, or the form, which is projected onto the raw material.

A sculpture, for example, may be made out of clay — its *chomer* — but its *tzurah* is the specific form that it takes. The *chomer* of a table is wood, for example, and its *tzurah* is the structure itself.

The concepts of *chomer* and *tzurah* are found not only in physical entities, but in deeper aspects of human experience as well.

In the parent/child relationship, often it is the mother who nurtures the child, giving birth to and sustaining his *chomer*, and the father who disciplines him and molds his raw material in a specific way, thereby creating his *tzurah*.

God, of course, is the ultimate *Tzurah* (as He imprints His will onto everything), and the entire world is His *chomer*.

Within God's creation, the physical elements are *chomer* and man is their *tzurah* (as he forms them into useful things).

Even among human beings, there are those who are mostly *chomer* and those who are mostly *tzurah*. A *chomer* person contains within himself much human ability, but is easily influenced by others. A *tzurah* personality, on the other hand, imprints his influence on other people and molds their character but is not influenced by others. A king, for example, is a *tzurah* personality who imprints his will and character onto the people in his nation.

Thus, it is clear why Yosef, from among all of Avraham's descendants, had a consummate *tzurah* personality: As the firstborn of Rachel (the preferred wife of Yaakov), he was destined for a royal leadership role.

Yet even someone who develops a *tzurah* personality of royalty and leadership later in life, and impresses his will upon others in very significant ways, is, in his youth, still subject to being impacted upon by other people. (His own personality has not yet fully emerged.) Moreover, as a young person, his physical desires (his *chomer* aspect) generally dictate the pursuits of his mind (his *tzurah* aspect), and not the other way around.

Yosef entered Egypt as a teenager, at a point in his life when his *tzurah* personality lay dormant. He was in a *chomer* state, which found expression in his being sold as a slave and then being thrown into jail. A slave is the epitome of *chomer*; he cannot imprint his will onto anything or anyone else, but is subjugated by others. A slave in jail even more so.

Only when he reached the age of thirty did Yosef's *tzurah* potential emerge fully. It was then that, in quick succession, he left the dungeon, shook of the grime and dirt of his imprisonment, and in a matter of days, rose to the position of viceroy of the entire land of Egypt.

The Jewish People as a Parallel to Yosef

The Jewish People are a *tzurah* people. Their role is to impress, onto all of humanity, goodness and Godliness.

The Jews' experience as a nation followed the pattern of Yosef's life — a period of *chomer* followed by the emergence of *tzurah*. In the beginning of the Jewish People's development into a nation, they were slaves (*chomer*) in Egypt. Not only were they enslaved, but they were afflicted by their masters — their entire character, personality, and value system (their *tzurah*) was subjugated. But at a time determined by God, their *tzurah* aspect emerged; it was then that they left Egypt, accepted the Torah, and marched into the Land of Israel to become a light unto the nations and to impress absolute morality onto mankind.

Yosef's Nature

We have seen that Yosef was destined for a *tzurah* role of leadership. But why specifically over the land of Egypt?

Egypt was a land steeped in sexual immorality. This is evident from several accounts in the Torah. When Avraham had gone down to Egypt years before during a famine, he had been so afraid of his wife Sarah's abduction that he had hidden her in a box.

Many years later, before the Jews entered the Land of Israel, God said to them: "You must not act in the [same] manner as [the Egyptians] [referring to the decadent behavior that the Egyptians engaged in]..." (*Vayikra* 18:3).

Every human being is comprised of two parts: a body and a soul. The body is the *chomer* aspect of the person; the soul is the *tzurah*.

When man allows his soul to control his body, his *tzurah* dominates. When he uses his body to control his soul (specifically, by engaging in sexual deviancy), his *chomer* prevails.

Egypt, a land mired in immorality, determined its societal values by the desires of its collective "body." Egypt was a nation of *chomer*.

Yosef epitomized the antithesis of Egypt. Not only would he not engage in sexual wrongdoing, but even when Potiphar's wife tried to seduce him (changing her clothing several times a day to attract him[1]), he overcame her advances. This, even though he was hundreds of miles away from his father's influence.

Yosef was a consummate *tzurah*, whose soul imprinted its will, very clearly, onto his body.[2]

Egypt was the quintessential *chomer* land, Yosef the quintessential *tzurah* personality. Yosef, as Egypt's spiritual counterforce, was perfectly suited to fill the vacuum that Egypt presented. He

---

1. *Yoma* 35b.
2. It was mentioned above that Yosef's *tzurah* potential did not fully awaken until he reached the age of thirty. Apparently, however, even in his *chomer* state, Yosef had enough of a *tzurah* personality to withstand the temptation and advances of Potiphar's wife.

thus became the one to mold the character of the nation.³

The Ten Donkeys and the Ten Asses

The Torah recounts how, a number of years later, Yosef's brothers came down to Egypt. After a series of events, Yosef revealed his identity to them, and assured them that he did not bear a grudge against them for selling him into slavery so many years before. It was destined, he told them, that he be sold into Egypt as a slave, so that he would be able to provide food for the family, in the years of hunger.⁴

The Torah then tells us that Yosef sent along with his brothers ten (male) donkeys loaded with gifts for his father, and ten asses (female donkeys) loaded with food for their journey back to the Land of Israel. Why did Yosef send donkeys for his father and asses for his brothers? And why did he give each *ten* animals?

With the different animals, Yosef was sending different messages to his father and to his brothers.

To his father, Yosef wanted to convey that he understood that the family had to come down to Egypt to fulfill what God had told Avraham in the *Bris Bein Habesarim*, and that he saw his ten brothers who had sold him as the *vehicle* (a donkey is known as a "beast of burden") that brought this about. A donkey carries a load to its destination, which is controlled by the rider. Similarly, the brothers acted as they did and sold him into slavery, but they had no control over his final destination, that being in God's hands. Thus, he bore no grudge against them.

---

3. *Gevuros Hashem*, chapter 11.

The Midrash implies that Yosef made Egypt a more moral place during his reign. It teaches (*Bereshis Rabbah* 90:6) that Yosef, as viceroy, made all of the Egyptian males undergo circumcision. Many commentaries explain circumcision as symbolizing limitation of and control over man's sexual drive (see Rabbi Shimshon Refael Hirsch on *Bereshis* 17:10). Yosef, as a *tzurah*, forced the Egyptians to exercise self-control and morality, in contrast to their free and immoral lives.

4. cf. *Bereshis* 45:5.

To his brothers, however, Yosef sent a different, gentler, message with the ten asses. In this case he was likening himself to a female donkey. Just as a female donkey nurses its young, he was destined to provide sustenance for the family during the difficult years of famine. This, Yosef was reassuring his brothers, was the true reason that he had to be sold into slavery in Egypt.[5]

Yosef's Journey into Slavery

Yosef was sold a number of times before he was finally sold to Potiphar the landowner in Egypt.

Rav Yudan says: *"He was first sold to Ishmaelites, and was then resold to [Ishmaelite] traders. The traders then sold him to Midianites, who in turn resold him to [Potiphar] in Egypt."*

Rav Huna says (*Midrash Rabbah* 84:20): *"In Egypt, he was first sold to [the head of a government agency (who bought him for official use)],*[6] *and he [sold Yosef] to Potiphar."*

Why was it necessary for Yosef to pass through so many hands before he was brought to Egypt? What is the deeper meaning of his being sold and resold so many times?

Yosef was being led from the bosom of the most sublime and spiritual family in the world into slavery in Egypt, the most decadent civilization of the time. It was proper that he not go from such a high level to such a low level directly, but rather to descend in a series of small gradations.

Yosef was first sold to Ishmaelites. Ishmael was not an entirely bad person. He was Avraham's son, and emulated the *chesed* of his father. He did *teshuvah* at the end of his life, and his progeny is seen as worthy of being listed in the Torah.

He was then sold to Ishmaelite *traders*. Traders buy from and sell to people from other communities. Because they travel and therefore have dealings with other more decadent people, Ishmaelite traders represent the fringe element of the Ishmaelite

---

5. *Gevuros Hashem*, chapter 10.
6. As a CEO would buy a "company car."

people. Therefore, Yosef's being sold to the traders was a step further away from his origins.

He was then sold to a group of Midianites. The nation of Midian was spawned from the progeny of Avraham and his last wife, Keturah. They were more distant from the Jewish People, both physically and spiritually, than were the Ishmaelite traders. This represented a further step down for Yosef.

Finally, Yosef was sold to an Egyptian, a member of a morally degenerate people. This was the furthest possible point from the spirituality that he had experienced in his father's home in the Land of Israel.

* * *

Rav Huna says that Yosef was sold to an Egyptian government official before he was sold to Potiphar. Why this added step?

A slave owned by a corporation, and certainly by a government agency, is not as controlled as a slave who is owned by a single person. A slave without a specific owner cannot be subjugated as profoundly, because there is no distinct chain of command for him to follow. This was Yosef's first level of slavery.

From there he was sold to Potiphar, an individual who gave Yosef definite instructions and imprinted his will directly upon him. This was a much deeper level of slavery.[7]

---

7. *Gevuros Hashem*, chapter 11.

4
The Ten Plagues

WHEN GOD DECIDED TO bring the slavery of the Jews in Egypt to a close, He could have simply inspired the Egyptians to voluntarily free the Jews. But He did not: Instead he afflicted the Egyptians with ten[1] plagues and *forced* them to free the Jews. The Ten Plagues accomplished two things: They punished the Egyptians for tormenting the Jews during the many years of enslavement, and they showed the Egyptians, the Jews, and the entire world that God controlled every aspect of creation.[2]

The Ten Plagues were:
(1) Blood (2) Frogs (3) Lice (4) Wild Animals (5) Pestilence (the death of the Egyptians' domestic animals) (6) Boils (7) Hail (8) Locusts (9) Darkness (10) Death of the Egyptian Firstborn.

---

1. The number ten is very significant. As mentioned in chapter 2, the philosophical meaning of the number ten is "a unity created from many individual parts."

There are Ten Commandments because the entire message of God at Sinai was divided into ten different commandments. The world was created with ten Divine Statements, because the entire experience of creation had ten segments to it.

There were ten plagues for this reason too: Through ten actions, God showed the world that He controls every aspect of nature. All together, the plagues express that God controls the world.

2. Perhaps this was accomplished most effectively in Egypt, because it was the most technologically advanced country at that time and claimed a divine king.

* * *

Is there any significance to the *order* of the Ten Plagues? And were the plagues meaningful in and of themselves, or were they just different ways of punishing the Egyptians?

If, as we have stated, the purpose of the plagues was to show that God controls all of nature (and this was the one time in history that God chose to reveal His hand so openly), then, without doubt, the *way* that God demonstrated His dominion over creation must have followed a meaningful order.

The physical world can be broken down into three levels of creation:

1. The "bottom level" — earth and water
2. The "top level" — sun, moon, and stars
3. The "middle level" — human beings and animals (who live between the earth and the sky)

Through the Ten Plagues, God showed His control over all three parts of creation.

The first three plagues expressed God's dominion over the "bottom level" of creation: The plagues of blood and frogs affected the water (the Nile River[3]), and the plague of lice affected the dust of the earth.

The second three plagues demonstrated God's dominion over the "middle level" of creation: Wild beasts, pestilence, and boils affected people and animals.

The third set of plagues showed God's dominion over the "top level" of creation: Hail, locusts, and darkness all come from above.

The tenth plague expressed God's control over something even loftier than all three levels of the physical world: It exhibited His control over the human *soul*, representing His total control over the entire *meta*physical world.[4]

---

3. In the second plague, the Nile spawned hordes of frogs that covered Egypt.
4. Interestingly, the *Bris Bein Habesarim* also reflected this pattern of three times three plus one. (See chapter 2.)

Three Sets of Three

According to the above-mentioned explanation, the Ten Plagues were composed of three sets of three plagues, plus one final plague. Within each group of three plagues, was there any significance to their order?

As mentioned before, the numbers one, two, and three have deep, philosophical meanings. The number one represents unity, oneness, and Divinity. The number two represents expansion and diversity.[5] And the number three represents the point where the diversity of two embraces an underlying common theme, which unites them.[6] Indeed, each set of three plagues follows this pattern, as the first two plagues represent opposing occurrences, and the third plague represents an occurrence that blends the first two together.[7]

The First Three Plagues

In light of the above, we can understand the first three plagues thus:

Blood is a hot liquid,[8] and frogs inhabit cool water; hot and cold represent polar opposites. Lice grow in warm, damp places, however, which represents a fusion of hot and cold.

---

5. One and two are polar opposites.
6. We find this concept in another regard, too. The defining character trait of Avraham was *chesed* (generosity, going beyond the call of duty). The defining character trait of Yitzchak was *din* (judgment, living life precisely, exactly within the call of duty). The defining character trait of Yaakov was *emes*, truth. Truth encompasses both of the above two traits, as it determines when it is correct to act within the call of duty and when to act beyond it.
7. Similarly, Pharaoh was warned to free the Jews (or risk punishment) before the first two plagues of each set, but he was not warned before the third. As the third plague in each set was a synthesis of the two plagues that preceded it, it did not warrant the verbalization of a new warning.
8. That is, live blood inside a human body.

In showing His control over two opposites, and a fusion of the two, God showed His full control over the entire "hot-to-cold" paradigm in creation: over the "hot," the "cold," and everything in between.

The Second Set of Plagues

Wild animals appearing suddenly in inhabited areas and killing human beings is an unnatural occurrence.[9] Animals dying by disease (pestilence), however, is quite natural; it happens regularly. As with the first set of plagues, these two events represent polar opposites, and boils represent a middle point between the two; boils are not an everyday occurrence, but are not extraordinary either.

In showing control over two extremes and then a combination of the two, God showed His full control over the entire spectrum of events that occur: the ordinary, extraordinary, and everything in between.

The Third Three Plagues

Hail originates in the heavens and falls to the ground. Locusts fly from the ground to the sky. Again, these are polar opposites. Darkness occurs when the sun is obscured, the sun being something that (to the human observer) travels from the earth to the sky and then back again — expressing a fusion of the previous two plagues. This third set of plagues thus expressed God's control over the entire "motion" spectrum of this world.

As mentioned before, the tenth plague represents God's control over something greater than any paradigm that exists in the physical world: His control over the metaphysical world, illustrated by his taking the souls of the Egyptian firstborn.

The Punishment Aspect of the Ten Plagues

Let us now return to the first reason we cited for God's bringing

---

9. See *Gevuros Hashem*, chapter 57.

the Ten Plagues: to punish the Egyptians for the suffering they had brought upon the Jews during their years of enslavement.

The plagues were not equal in severity; rather, they formed a progression in which each successive plague came closer to attacking the souls of the Egyptians.

The first three plagues were terribly unpleasant occurrences for the Egyptians, but were not life-threatening. The plague of blood was mitigated by the fact that the Egyptians could purchase water from the Jews (*Shemos Rabbah* 9:10). And both the frogs and lice were unpleasant and unsettling, but did not threaten the Egyptians' lives in any way.

The fourth, fifth, and sixth plagues were significantly more dangerous. The wild animals on the loose killed anyone who ventured out of his house; pestilence wiped out all domestic animals (even those in the protected stables); and the boils disfigured the Egyptians bodily, in a most painful and humiliating way.

The third set of plagues brought even more severe punishment: hail destroyed almost all the crops and was accompanied by earth-shattering noises[10] that scared the Egyptians almost to death.[11] Locusts ate up whatever produce was left in the fields, threatening the Egyptians with extinction (in fact, it was the only plague called "death" by the Egyptians[12]). And the plague of darkness included three days of thick, paralyzing atmosphere in which the Egyptians literally could not move — an entombing, death-like experience.

Finally, the tenth plague attacked the very core of the Egyptians: It brought actual death to the Egyptian firstborn.

The Hardening of Pharaoh's Heart

Yet another perspective on the patterns formed by the Ten Plagues in contained in the Torah. This approach will not divide

---

10. *Shemos* 9:23.
11. See *Gevuros Hashem*, chapter 57.
12. *Shemos* 10:17.

them into three sets of three plus one, but into two sets of five plagues.

The Torah tells us that after each of the first five plagues, Pharaoh refused to free the Jews from Egypt. Yet after each of the second five plagues, Pharaoh *would have* freed the Jews had God not hardened his heart and not allowed him to do so (in order to complete the punishment due Pharaoh). Why was it that the first five plagues could not break Pharaoh's resolve, but the second five plagues could?

The difference between the first five plagues and the second five plagues was that whereas the first five plagues affected things that existed on the low or middle "level" of creation, the last five plagues affected things that existed on the "high level" of creation — or affected man directly.

The first plague turned the water (low level) of Egypt into blood; the sixth plague covered man (affecting man directly) with bloody boils.

The second plague "opened" the sea (low level) and flooded the land of Egypt with frogs; the seventh plague opened the heavens (high level) and poured hail down onto man.

The third plague had lice (low level) crawl up out of the earth and inundate Egypt; the eighth plague had locusts (high level) fly down and cover Egypt.[13]

The fourth plague had wild animals (middle level), who normally attack people only at night, attack during the day; the ninth plague brought darkness (high level), which normally occurs only at night, during the day as well.[14]

---

13. While the lice crawled onto man, they originated in the ground. The locusts destroyed the crops as they swooped in from the sky.

14. An additional thought: the plague of wild animals was called ערוב (from ערב/mixture) because there was a mix of wild animals in Egypt. Evening is called ערב too, as it begins with twilight, the mixture of night and day when one cannot distinguish between different objects. Morning is called בקר because one is able to be מבקר/notice differences between things.

The fifth plague killed the domestic animals (middle level); the tenth plague killed the firstborn Egyptians (affecting man directly).

Since the first five plagues only affected the low and middle levels of Egypt, Pharaoh was able to withstand them, and thus did not feel forced to free the Jews. The last five plagues, however, affected the higher levels of creation, including man. This was unbearable for Pharaoh, and he would have freed the Jews had God not hardened his heart, thus not allowing him to do so.

5
The Exodus

ALTHOUGH THE EXODUS from Egypt was a one-time occurrence in Jewish history, it plays a pivotal role in the definition of the Jewish People and its mission. This is apparent in the following way:

There are three major holidays mentioned in the Torah: Pesach, Shavuos, and Sukkos. The Torah tells us that all three of them are related to our Exodus from Egypt.

When the Torah mentions Pesach, it says the following verse: *"You shall observe... and... carry out the pesach-sacrifice [before] the Eternal, your God... [Who] took you out of Egypt at night"* (*Devarim* 16:1).

When Shavuos is discussed, the Torah says, *"You shall then observe the [Shavuos] festival [before] the Eternal... [And] you shall remember that you were [once] a slave in Egypt"* (Devarim 16:10,12).

Regarding Sukkos, the Torah includes the following verse: *"[You shall dwell in sukkos]...so that your [succeeding] generations will be aware that I settled the Children of Israel in booths when I took them out of...Egypt"* (*Vayikra* 23:43).

Even Shabbos, the weekly "holiday," is intristically connected to the Exodus from Egypt, The Torah states: *"You shall remember that you were [once] a slave in the land of Egypt, but God...brought you out from there...therefore God has commanded you to observe the Shabbos day"* (*Devarim* 5:15).

Furthermore, every Jew is commanded to remember the Exodus every single day, as it says: *"[You shall] remember the day you left the land of Egypt all the days of your life"* (*Devarim* 16:3). The mitzvos of mezuzah and tefillin are related to our Exodus from Egypt as well.

What is it about the Exodus that is so central to our beliefs and our practices?

Interestingly, it is not the great miracles that took place throughout the Exodus that are the basis of the holidays, Shabbos, or the commandments. There is no holiday or commandment that commemorates the Ten Plagues or the splitting of the Red Sea — perhaps the two greatest miracles that our people have ever witnessed. It is the Exodus itself — the transformation of our people from slaves to a free nation chosen by God to promulgate His will to humanity — that is the root of our observance. We celebrate our responsibilities to God and to the world; not the fact that God, in His kindness, suspended nature on our behalf to perform great miracles.

Let us now take a moment to understand more deeply the significance of our freedom from slavery — that is, what actually occurred when we were transformed from slaves into free people.

The Torah illustrates the process of our freedom from slavery with two analogies:

1. *"The Eternal brought you out of the iron furnace, Egypt, to be His designated people"* (*Devarim* 4:20).
2. *"Did any god perform such miracles, to come [and] take for himself one nation from the midst of [another] nation, with trials, signs [and] wonders... [as God took you out of Egypt]?"* (*Devarim* 4:34).

The Midrash[1] expounds on the meaning of these two verses:

1. *"The Eternal brought you out of the iron furnace, Egypt, to be His designated people"*: God took us out of Egypt as a goldsmith takes gold out of a sweltering pot.
2. *"One nation from the midst of [another] nation"*: Said Rabbi

---

1. *Shachar Tov* (*Tehillim* 114).

Abba bar Acha in the name of Rabbi Channa: God took the Jewish people out of Egypt as [a shepherd] pulls an [animal] fetus out of its mother's womb.

Let us now compare these two analogies to the Jews' enslavement — and their subsequent freedom.

The Egyptians enslaved the Jews in two ways.

1. They controlled their physical movements by not allowing them to move about freely, and by forcing them to serve in slave labor brigades.
2. They distanced the Jews with Egyptian culture and values, and enstranged them from their own traditions. Even if the Jews could have, theoretically, found a way to escape Egypt, they would never have even thought of it, as they were not capable of seeing themselves as an independent entity separate from Egypt. This "slave mentality" was as much a part of their enslavement as the physical oppression.

When God freed us from slavery in Egypt, He undid both aspects of our enslavement.

1. Just as a smith takes boiling hot gold out of a sweltering cauldron, so did God take the Jews out of the chains that had bound them. The Egyptians created barriers that denied the Jews free movement, much as fire and heat lock in the gold in a furnace. God took the Jews out of their bonds, just as a smith expertly extracts gold from between the smoke and flames.
2. Just as a shepherd takes a fetus out of its mother's womb, so did God free the Jews from the "slave mentality" that made freedom an incomprehensible concept. A fetus does not have an identity of its own; it is contained within its mother. Only when it leaves the womb does it become an independent entity. The Jews in Egypt lacked their own identity; when God freed them, they broke out of their psychological and emotional shackles to become their own

masters in every way.

The Two Aspects of Enslavement

There are two aspects to every nation:
1. The raw material, or *chomer* — i.e. the nation's multitudes of people.
2. The personality and character, or *tzurah* — i.e. the culture that imprints its values onto the individuals in the nation.

The Torah says that the Egyptians *enslaved* and *afflicted*[2] the Jewish People. Perhaps these two words are telling us that the Egyptians subjugated both the *chomer* and the *tzurah* aspects of the Jewish People.

The word "enslaved" means that the multitudes of Jews were forced to work in slave labor brigades — performing backbreaking, crushing labor. This refers to domination over the *chomer* aspect of the Jewish People.

The word "afflicted" refers to something else. It means that the Egyptians tried to break the spirit and character of the Jews in a conscious attempt to demoralize them and break their *tzurah*, or national character.

* * *

The two aforementioned verses (*The Eternal brought you out of the iron furnace, Egypt, to be His designated people*, and *God [took you] for Himself, a nation from the midst of another nation*) may also be addressing the *chomer* and *tzurah* aspects of our slavery.

The first verse says that God freed us from Egypt to become a chosen nation for Him. "A chosen nation" is a definition of our national character, an implication of our *tzurah* being freed from Egypt.

The second verse says that God took a nation out from amongst another nation. Literally, this means that God undid the shackles that kept us in Egypt and allowed us to go free, an impli-

---

2. *Shemos* 1:12–13.

cation of freeing the multitudes or *chomer* of our people.³

The Number 600,000

As mentioned earlier (chapter 1), our patriarch Avraham could not receive the Torah because it could only be given to a nation, and not to an individual. God therefore waited until Avraham's descendants developed into a nation, and then gave them the Torah.

The Jews reached the status of a nation when they totaled a sum of 600,000 righteous⁴ men, or households,⁵ who were between twenty and sixty years of age.

Clearly, the number 600,000 is crucial to the status of a nation. But how is that?

The number six is related to the concept of completion. A simple one-dimensional line extends in two directions. A flat square is two-dimensional and extends in four directions. A box-shaped item is three-dimensional and extends in six directions — the

---

3. The *chomer/tzurah* aspects of our enslavement in Egypt and subsequent redemption are alluded to in *Tehillim* 114 as well. There, King David says: "When *Yisrael* went out of Egypt, the *House of Yaakov* from a people of strange language..."

Two titles are given to the Jews after they were freed from Egypt: Yisrael and Yaakov. "Yaakov" (a derivative of the Hebrew word עקב, meaning "heel," the part of the body that touches the ground) refers to freeing the *chomer* of the Jewish People. "Yisrael," which is the name that captures the spiritual *mission* of the Jewish People as God's ambassadors to humanity (see *Chullin* 92a and the Malbim on *Yeshayahu* 40:27), refers to the character and *tzurah* of our people.

Both the *chomer* and the *tzurah* of our people were enslaved, and both were redeemed by God.

4. Eighty percent of the Jewish People died in the plague of darkness because they were not righteous (*Mechilta, Beshalach* 1:18). The remainder totaled 600,000, and were the righteous core of the righteous Jewish People.

5. The women were not counted. The assumption is that every man over twenty was married, and that each man represented a family unit.

highest number possible in the physical world. For that matter, something that extends in six directions —though it may be small — is more expressive of wholeness and completion than something that appears in two or four directions, even if it is large in size. Thus, in this world, the number six represents wholeness, as it represents every direction in which an entity can exist.

It is fitting for the Jewish People to be a nation whose core number is six. The Jewish People are a people apart. We cannot mesh permanently with any other nation. We are set apart from the rest of humanity because we have a mission that is different from theirs. Since we cannot connect with any other nation, we are complete, whole, on our own.[6] It therefore follows that the Jewish People became a nation when their number of righteous family units totaled a number which is a multiple of six — the number expressive of wholeness.

---

6. The other nations are not complete, as they are only a part of the greater humanity.

6
Sinai

THE TORAH WAS GIVEN to the Jewish People at Mount Sinai, in the month of Sivan. As with every aspect of Torah, the time in which the Torah was given is very significant.

In the Third Month

In our mystical tradition, every number has symbolic meaning. The number one represents unity, wholeness, and Godliness. The number two represents separation, disunity, and multiplicity. And the number three represents a connection between two disparate entities; a common theme that unites the two. For example, two lines connected at a point may extend in different directions, but a third line unites them to form a single triangle. Two separate bricks may share no common purpose, but a third brick placed on top of them will unify them into a building unit. A chair with only two legs will topple over, but with a third leg it can stand.

The number three, then, expresses the concept of connection and unification of disparate entities. As we will soon see, this is the key to understanding why it was appropriate for the Torah to have been given in the third month, Sivan.

The Midrash (*Koheles Rabbah* 3:1) comments on the verse לכל זמן ועת לכל חפץ תחת השמים — "For everything there is a set time, and a moment for each object beneath the heavens" (*Koheles* 3:1): "For everything there is a time (זמן): There was an exact time for Adam to enter the Garden of Eden — and to leave it. There was an exact time for Noach to enter the Ark — and to leave it. A moment (עת) for each object: There was an exact time for the Torah to be given to the Jews at Sinai."

Notice that King Solomon, the author of *Koheles*, uses two different words for *time*: זמן and עת. The word זמן means time in the general sense, and the word עת means time in the active or present tense (from the word עתה/now).

The Midrash uses the term זמן when referring to the events of Adam and Noach, and the term עת when referring to the time when the Jews were given the Torah. The distinction is significant.

There are three dimensions of time: the past, the present, and the future. The past can be easily recorded, as it encompasses a finite span of time. The future can be envisioned too, although its events are not yet known. But there is no moment that can be identified as "the present." It is so fleeting that as soon as it has been labeled "the present" it has become part of "the past." The present is the dimension of time least attached to the physical world, as it cannot be quantified.[1] Expressed differently, it is "metaphysical," and only serves to connect the past and the future.

The events of Adam and Noach are termed זמן in the Midrash because they related to the development of man in the physical world. Adam's entry into the Garden of Eden and his departure from it were part of the physical experience of mankind. Noach's entering and leaving the ark was also related to the unfolding of the story of mankind.

The giving of the Torah, however — the ultimate metaphysical entity in this world — is described in the *midrash* with the word עת (the present). Since the Torah is metaphysical, the word used for the "time" of its giving is the one that relates to a dimen-

---

1. Things that can be defined in physical terms are more connected to the physical world, and things that cannot be quantified are less physical. See page 87 for a discussion on a related topic.

sion least attached to the physical world. Accordingly, the Torah was given in a time that was related to the "metaphysical" present. The present serves as a "connector of two disparate parts" (the past and the future); it is thus closely connected to the number "three." Therefore, it was fitting for the Torah to be given in Sivan, the month that expresses the dimension of three.[2]

Not surprisingly, the constellation of Sivan, the third month, is *twins*: two separate people who share a unique oneness. That is exactly the message of the number three: a common theme that transcends and joins a dichotomy of two.[3]

Given on Shabbos

The Midrash says that the Torah was given on Shabbos.

On Shabbos, creative work is prohibited — yet creative spiritual work (which is accomplished by performing mitzvos) is permitted. Shabbos is a spiritual day, not connected to the physical world. It is thus fitting that Torah, the ultimate metaphysical entity, should be given on Shabbos.[4]

* * *

The first Shabbos in history brought creation to completion. It is fitting that Torah, the absolute moral guide intended to bring the world to perfection, should also be given on Shabbos.[5]

---

2. The giving of the Torah is connected to the number three in other ways, too. The Talmud (*Shabbos* 88a) says: "The Torah was given to the third, by the third, on the third, in the third month." It was given to Moshe (the third born in his family), on the third day [as it says "Be prepared, for on the third day (of preparation) God will descend upon Mount Sinai (*Shemos* 19:11)], in the third month, Sivan.

3. *Tiferes Yisrael*, chapter 25.

4. *Tiferes Yisrael*, chapter 27.

5. Maharal's exact words are יום שבת הוא השלמת העולם. In a deeper way, the Shabbos brings a level of completion to the world every week.

Fifty Days after the Exodus

The Talmud (*Rosh Hashanah* 21b) says that there are fifty levels of spirituality, with the fiftieth level being totally sublime, beyond any connection to the physical world.

The Torah was given fifty days after the Jewish People left Egypt; the fifty-day waiting period enabled the Jews to ascend to the highest (fiftieth) level, in order to be able to connect to the Torah.

In the Counting of the Omer (the days from Passover until Shavuos), only forty-nine days are counted. The fiftieth day (Shavuos) is not part of the calculation. This is because the fiftieth day represents the fiftieth level of spirituality — the *entirely* sublime — and it cannot be grouped together with the other forty-nine days, as they have at least some amount of physicality within them.

This ascent in spirituality is noted in another way, too. The Omer offering brought on the first of the fifty days (the 16th day of Nissan) was made of barley, a coarse food used to feed animals. The *Shtei Halechem* offering, brought on the fiftieth day (the 6th of Sivan), was made out of pure wheat, a substance of the highest quality. This too symbolized the transition of the Jews to a higher level.

The Desert

The Midrash says[6]: "בשלשה דברים נתנה התורה: באש במים במדבר: *The Torah was given in the presence of three things: fire, water,[7] and the desert.*"

We have seen that the time the Torah was given is significant. The place where it was given is important, too. Just as the Torah was given in the least physical dimension of time, it was given in the least physical kind of place.

---

6. *Bemidbar Rabbah* 1:7.

7. The heavy clouds that surrounded Mount Sinai (*Shemos* 19:16) rained water onto the mountain (*Bemidbar Rabbah* 1:17).

Things that can be "owned" have physical borders, and are firmly rooted in the physical world. A field, for example, can be owned because it has defined borders, and encompasses an exact amount of space. But things that do not have borders are less rooted in the physical world and cannot be owned by anyone.

Indeed, within the physical world there are entities that can be owned, and entities that defy ownership.

The three things with which the Torah was given — fire, water, and the desert — cannot be "owned" by anyone. Fire is available to everyone (anyone can create a fire with two stones); it is therefore less physical than other creations. Water is also widely available, and no one can truly claim to own it. In this sense it is less physical too. The desert naturally defies ownership; it discourages habitation, as it does not grow food or provide sustenance for animals or humans. Thus: fire, water, and the desert, the most "non-physical" of the physical elements, created the most appropriate backdrop for the giving of the Torah.[8]

An Alternative Explanation

There is another explanation with which to understand the relationship of fire, water, and desert to Torah. The Torah's moral code contains two opposite kinds of actions: mitzvos — instructions on how to positively relate to God and humanity; and *aveiros* — transgressions of those principles. The Torah tells us that one who performs mitzvos will be tremendously rewarded, and one who commits *aveiros* will be severely punished. Perhaps fire, water, and the desert were present at the giving of the Torah because they represent three different aspects of Torah.

Fire expresses the *aveiros* in the Torah. An *aveirah* is a bad deed in the absolute value system of the Torah. Its punishment is absolute, too, a concept commonly represented by fire, perhaps the most devastating of natural phenomena.[9]

---

8. *Tiferes Yisrael*, chapter 26.
9. For this reason, *Gehinom* (hell) is associated with fire.

Water represents the mitzvos in the Torah: Water is the basic building block of civilizations, bringing life wherever it flows. Mitzvos bring eternal life as reward for their performance.

The desert represents the nature of Torah itself. Torah is metaphysical, totally different from the physical creation; the desert is the most non-physical environment possible. Torah was thus given in the desert.

The Name Shavuos

The Torah calls the holiday of Shavuos by two names: חג האסיף/ The Festival of Harvest and חג השבועות/The Festival of Weeks. However, in our prayers, we refer to Shavuos by a different name: זמן מתן תורתנו/The time of the giving of our Torah. Why doesn't the Torah refer to Shavuos as "the time of the giving of the Torah," a seemingly more fitting name (as it describes the function of the day)? And why do we refer to Shavuos by a name that is not mentioned in the Torah?

Consider: A festival is a day that commemorates a crucial experience of the Jewish People. Shavuos commemorates the giving of the Torah, which includes within it both reward and punishment. The Torah is "for keeps," as one who is not careful to follow its dictates is held accountable for it. In fact, the Midrash says that the other nations thought that the Torah would be too hard to keep, and therefore rejected it.[10] God, then, could not have called Shavuos "a festival of the Torah" if the majority of humanity did not see the Torah as something desirable. Instead, He called it חג האסיף, The Festival of Harvest, and חג השבועות, The Festival of Weeks.

The Jewish People, however, understand that accepting the Torah has given them the ability to connect with God in the deepest way, and affords them the most meaningful human experience possible. They understand that the Torah, while difficult, is eternally beneficial. Therefore, they can, and do, refer to Shavuos

---

10. *Mechilta, Yisro* 5:2.

as "the time of the giving of the Torah."[11]

To Each Man an Angel

At Mount Sinai, when the Jewish People accepted God's offer of the Torah, they called out *"na'aseh venishma — We will carry out [God's will], and [only then will we] heed [understand] everything"* (*Shemos* 24:7). The Jews committed themselves to fulfilling the mitzvos even before they knew what those mitzvos would be.

The saying of *na'aseh venishma* was a tremendous merit for the Jewish People, as it indicated their belief in the goodness of the Torah, because of their absolute belief in the goodness of God. The Talmud (*Shabbos* 88a) tells us of the great reward the Jews received: Each Jew received two crowns from God, One for *na'aseh* and one for *nishma*. A separate angel was dispatched to give out each crown, because the Midrash (*Bereshis Rabbah* 50:2) teaches, "One angel cannot do two missions simultaneously." Yet, wasn't the act of giving the crowns to the Jews one general mission? Why were separate angels needed for each person, and for each crown?

The answer lies in appreciating the importance of each person in the Jewish Nation. If a population of no less than 600,000 men (or family units) was needed to form our identity as a nation, then each individual in that group was clearly an indispensable part of that nation. Clearly, each member added his own dimension to the national character.

Each Jew is immeasurably unique. Therefore, each statement of "we will do and we will hear" was said from a unique perspective and outlook. Each reward, then, would have to be unique too, to correspond exactly to the action done. Thus, no angel could give more than one crown to one person, as the giving of each crown was indeed a different mission.[12]

---

11. *Tiferes Yisrael*, chapter 28.
12. *Tiferes Yisrael*, chapter 30.

Twelve *Mil*

The Midrash (*Shabbos* 88b) says that when God spoke to the Jewish People at Mount Sinai, the entire nation flew back twelve *mil*,[13] and had to be brought back to the mountain by angels. Why twelve *mil*?

The Talmud says that the entire Jewish camp had a circumference of twelve *mil*.

The Jewish People, although they are God's emissaries, are still human beings and therefore can have no real relationship to the *essence* of God. Thus, when God spoke directly to the Jewish People at Mount Sinai, it was too much for them to bear. They could not remain where they were. Listening to God speak directly to them would be relating to Him in a way no human being could. They were distanced *the entire length* of the Jewish camp, implying that no part of the Jewish camp had any connection with God's essence at all.

Forced to Accept Torah

The Talmud (*Shabbos* 88a) says that when God revealed Himself to the Jewish People at Mount Sinai, He picked up the mountain, held it over their heads, and said: "If you accept my Torah, it will be good. If not, I will bury you here beneath this mountain." This statement is perplexing. The Jews had already accepted the Torah quite willingly, saying "we will do everything that God has said."[14] This expressed a total commitment to Torah. Why was it necessary for them to be forced to accept a Torah that they had already willingly accepted?

The role of the Jewish People is to teach humanity about God and His will. The Jewish People carry out this charge, to a great extent, by studying the Torah and practicing its laws. It is necessary, then, for the Jews and the Torah to be totally connected,

---

13. A *mil* equals about 1 km.
14. *Shemos* 19:8.

entirely joined.

When the Jews said, *"we will do and we will hear,"* they voluntarily chose a connection with Torah. A volunteer commitment based on goodwill is dependent on the continuation of that goodwill, and is therefore a weak, tenuous connection. For the Jewish People to be appointed as God's ambassadors, a much stronger and more durable connection was needed. Thus, God *forced* the Jews to accept Torah. A bond of force is free of the insecurities of choice. God's holding the mountain above the Jewish People shored up any unsteadiness that may have lain beneath their previous voluntary commitment.[15]

---

15. *Tiferes Yisrael*, chapter 32.

7
The Ten Commandments

FIFTY DAYS AFTER THE Jews left Egypt and crossed the Red Sea, God instructed them to gather around Mount Sinai. There, in the presence of fire, thunder, and smoke, God revealed Himself to them, and gave them the Ten Commandments.[1] The Ten Commandments were the first part of the Written Torah that God gave the Jewish People. The rest of the Torah was transmitted through Moshe at a later time.[2]

Why did God give us the Ten Commandments before He gave us the rest of the Torah? And do the Ten Commandments stand on their own in any way?

Connecting God to Man

There were two things that God accomplished by giving the Torah to the Jews. First, He established a relationship with them. Second, He gave them the practical instructions on how to come

---

1. In truth, they are not Ten *Commandments*, but rather Ten *Statements* (*dibros*). There are really thirteen commandments, as the second commandment contains four disparate instructions. We will use the term Ten Commandments, however, as it is understood to mean the information that God spoke at Sinai.

2. There is a disagreement in the Gemara (*Gittin* 60a) as to when the Torah was actually written down. Some say that it was given to Moshe in written form at Sinai, and others say that while the information was all given to Moshe at Sinai, the actual writing down of the Torah happened as the events occurred over the Jews' forty years in the desert.

close to Him within that relationship. The Torah provides the necessary framework for man to become more Godly, and, in turn, to make the world a more Godly place.

God could not have instructed the Jews to come close to Him before they understood that He was their God. The Jews first had to experience His existence as God. In hearing the Ten Commandments, the Jewish People heard God with their own ears and saw Him with their own eyes. They *experienced* His existence. A connection was forged. Once that connection was forged, the Jews could then be given instruction on how to strengthen that connection (the rest of the Torah). After the pathway was established through the Ten Commandments, the Jews could be told how to travel the path by keeping the 613 commandments.[3]

Aleph: The First Letter of the Ten Commandments

The "Torah" (which literally means "instruction") is God's instruction to man on how to live his life in this world. All that man could possibly need to know about the physical and mystical worlds, about morality and mortality, even about God Himself, is contained in the Torah. The Torah is the guidebook that the Cre-

---

3. *Tiferes Yisrael*, chapter 35.

The Talmud (*Shabbos* 88b) says that when the Jews heard the voice of God proclaim the first two commandments, they died from fright and had to be resuscitated by the angels. They then begged for God to tell Moshe the commandments and to have him impart the information to them.

Surely, God knew that the Jews could not hear the Ten Commandments directly from Him. Why, then, did He begin saying them at all?

It was crucial for the Jews to hear the "voice" of God directly. A person's most profound knowledge comes from things he has personally experienced. In order for the Jews to truly believe that the Torah was Divine, and to accept a mission to promulgate it to the world as Truth, they had to receive it directly from God, without an intermediary. Had the Jews only heard of Torah's Divine nature from Moshe, they could not have promoted its value system effectively, or with the same conviction.

ator wrote specifically for His primary creation, man.

Our tradition tells us that each letter of the Hebrew alphabet has a numerical value. *Aleph*, the first letter, has a numerical value of 1. It represents Oneness, Unity, and Godliness. The second letter of the alphabet is *beis*, which has a numerical value of 2, representing addition, expansion, and multiplicity.[4]

The Torah begins with a *beis* (בראשית), and the Ten Commandments begin with an *aleph* (אנכי). Let us try to understand why this is so.

The Torah begins with the story of Creation. Creation was a process of expansion. First, there was only God. Then He created myriad physical entities, which seemingly diversified the world into many parts. The story of Creation, then, is a story of addition, expansion, and multiplicity. That is why it begins with the letter *beis*.[5]

Through its mitzvos and ethical teachings, the Ten Commandments represent the law of the Torah.[6] The Torah provides a comprehensive framework within which we are commanded to

---

4. Even though all letters (besides *aleph*) have a multiple value, our tradition teaches that the first expression of a value (in this case the *beis*) always expresses that value most exactly. This concept is alluded to in *Bava Kamma* 55a, where it states that if one sees the letter *tes* in his dream, it is a sign of good things to come — as the first time the letter *tes* is used in the Torah is for the word *tov*, good (*Bereshis* 1:4). Thus, the essence of the letter *tes* is good. This concept is also discussed many times in the *Pri Tzaddik*, by Rabbi Tzadok ha-Kohen.

5. The Talmud (*Yerushalmi Chagigah* 2:2) teaches that *beis* represents the word ברכה (blessing). The root of the word ברכה is ברכ. Each of these letters represents multiplicity, as each is the first multiple in its numeric category: ב = 2 (the first multiple in the single digits), ר = 200 (the first in the hundreds), and כ = 20 (the first in the tens).

6. *Tiferes Yisrael*, chapter 35.

In fact, the commentaries say that the Ten Commandments contain the roots of all 613 commandments. See Rashi, in the name of Rav Sadya Gaon, on *Shemos* 24:12.

live. It is by living within this framework, we are taught, that we will bring creation closer to God.

Thus, the Torah is a metaphysical framework or structure that God instructed us to impose onto His multi-faceted creation. And structure, by definition, gives singularity to a multiplicity, because it allows many disparate parts to work together. That is why the Ten Commandments begin with the letter *aleph*: They represent the structure the Torah gives the world, the single goal and purpose with which God has endowed creation.

At One Moment

God then spoke all these words (*Shemos* 20:1): All of the commandments were said at one moment, something that a [human] mouth cannot say, and a [human] ear cannot hear. God first said the entire Ten Commandments [in one moment], and then repeated them individually, in the order that they are listed in the Torah (*Mechilta, Yisro* 4).

Why was it significant that God introduced the Ten Commandments by saying them all in one instant?

Consider: The purpose of the Torah is to create a unified structure that will express Godliness in the world, and teach us how to direct the surges of nature and mankind into that structure.

God is the source of all existence. Since everything is sourced in Him, He embodies unity.[7] It follows that if the ultimate unity is God, then the closer something is to God, the more it will express His unity. And the farther away an entity is from God, the less it will express His unity.[8]

The creation closest to God is the Torah (as it expresses His will). The part of Torah closest to God is the Ten Commandments,

---

7. As everything in creation shares a common source (God), it is God who unifies the entire creation.

8. Similarly, a person who reaches a high level of Godliness will exhibit an aura of wholeness and completion.

as it was the first part of the Torah God told to man.⁹

That is why the Ten Commandments were first said all at once. Because they are so connected to God, it was inevitable that they be said in unison. It was an expression of their closeness to the ultimate source of unity, God.¹⁰

The Ten Commandments

The Ten Commandments are:

1. I am the Eternal, your God.
2. You must not have any gods of others before me.
3. You must not swear by the name of the Eternal, your God, in vain.
4. Remember the Sabbath day so as to sanctify it.
5. Honor your father and your mother.
6. You must not murder.
7. You must not commit adultery.
8. You must not steal.
9. You must not give false testimony.
10. You must not desire the belongings of others.

As mentioned above, the Ten Commandments were the medium that forged a connection between the Jewish People and God. They contain laws on how to properly relate to both God and man. The commandments are divided into two sets of five

---

9. In our tradition, the first part of an entity encompasses the entire item. (The Ba'al haTanya and other commentaries write that the two days of Rosh Hashanah contain within them the future occurrences of the entire coming year.) Similarly, our tradition says that the entire Torah is rooted in the Ten Commandments (Rashi).

10. *Tiferes Yisrael*, chapter 34.

The fact that there are *Ten* Commandments also fits into this approach. The letter *yud* (which has a numerical value of 10) is written as a single dot — an entity which is unified, without parts, and which cannot be broken down (as other letters can).

Additionally, the *mispar kattan* (i.e. the sum of the digits of the number) of 10 is 1 (*Tiferes Yisrael*, chapter 35).

commandments each. The first set teaches us how to positively relate to God, and the second set teaches us how to properly relate to our fellowman.

The sequence of the commandments follows a very significant order.

The Order of the First Five Commandments

The first five commandments address different levels of our connection to God, beginning with the most fundamental and ending with the most distant aspect of our relationship to Him.

The first commandment orders us to believe that God exists. One who denies belief in God, denies God's very existence, and "assaults" His very essence.[11] This is the worst thing one can do in his relationship with God. This commandment is therefore listed fifth.

The second commandment forbids us to accept other gods. This requires us to believe in the *unity* of God. One who does accept multiple gods denies God's Singularity. This is not a denial of God's essence, but a denial of the fact that He is One. Therefore, it is listed second.

The third commandment orders us not to swear falsely in God's name. One who does not keep this commandment profanes God's name. This does not attack the essence or the unity of God. Rather, it violates God's *honor*. This is a step removed from the transgression of the second commandment. It is thus mentioned third.

The fourth commandment tells us to observe the Sabbath, a day that testifies that God created the world in six days and rested on the seventh. One who does not observe the Sabbath does not directly attack even God's honor. Rather, he denies the validity of a *witness* (the Sabbath day) that testifies that God created the world — an entity that relates to God's creation, rather than God Himself. The denial of God as Creator is one step removed from

---

11. Of course, in truth, man cannot affect God in any way.

violating His honor. Therefore, this commandment is listed fourth.[12]

The fifth commandment orders us to honor our father and mother. The Talmud (*Kiddushin* 30b) teaches that there are three partners in the creation of every person: the father, the mother, and God. One's parents are considered "partners" of God, and they represent Him much as a person's business partners represent him. One who fails to honor his parents thus negates a more distant aspect of his relationship with God. This commandment is therefore mentioned last.[13]

The Order of the Second Five Commandments

The second five commandments address man's relationship with his fellowman. Following the pattern of the first five commandments, they begin with the most serious affront to our fellowman and then descend in severity.

The first commandment in this set prohibits murder. Killing another person is clearly the worst thing one can do to him. It is therefore mentioned first.

The second commandment forbids adultery. Adultery destroys the "wholeness" of a person. The Torah sees man and woman as two halves of a whole, and an individual as complete only when he is together with his spouse. Since an adulterous woman may not remain married to her husband as a result of the adultery, both parties are denied the opportunity to become spiritually complete. This is a step less severe than murder, and is thus mentioned second.

The third commandment in this group, *lo signov*, refers specifically to kidnapping.[14] However, it can also be understood to include the general concept of theft.[15] Whereas adultery is an

---

12. *Tiferes Yisrael*, chapter 36.
13. Ibid.
14. See Rashi on *Shemos* 20:13.
15. See Maharal, *Tiferes Yisrael*, chapter 36.

assault on a person's *essence* (as it destroys his "completion"), theft is an assault on his *property*. In fact, even kidnapping, terrible though it is, does not attack the essence of a person. Rather, it limits his freedom of movement. This prohibition is therefore mentioned after the prohibition of adultery.

The fourth commandment forbids saying false testimony.[16] False testimony is, in essence, theft, as it causes damage to another person. It is, however, done in a less direct way than thievery itself. It is therefore mentioned after theft.

The fifth commandment forbids us to covet that which belongs to others. A person who wants something that belongs to his fellow allows his jealousy to affect his feelings towards that person. He may not directly hurt that person, but, in his own heart, his goodwill towards him suffers. This is a distant, more subtle assault on the essence of another human being. Thus, it is listed as the last of the second five commandments.[17]

The Ten Commandments at a Deeper Level

Let us now return to all Ten Commandments and study them individually,[18] with the goal of understanding them a bit more deeply.

The First Commandment

The first commandment is: *"I am the Eternal, your God, Who took you out of the land of Egypt, out of the house of slavery."*

A simple reading of this sentence seems to imply that it is merely a statement of God's existence. Is the first commandment

---

16. Even when not swearing in God's Name.
17. *Tiferes Yisrael*, chapter 36.

Of course, the above discussion has no basis in halachah. It is merely a philosophical explanation of the order of the first five commandments.

18. In our discussion, the first five commandments will be discussed individually, but the last five commandments will be addressed as a group.

commanding us to *do* anything, or is it merely an opening statement, a rationale for the commandments that follow?

Indeed, the first commandment is a *commandment*. The words "*I am your God*" mean: "See to it that I am your God. Relate to Me as your God. Affirm your belief in My Existence." However, if this is indeed the meaning of the commandment, then there must be a reason why it was not stated explicitly, as "Make Me your God."

The first commandment could not have been formulated as a direct commandment for two reasons.

First, a commandment is an instruction given by God to act in a certain way. Implicit in the command is that man has the free will to do or to disregard what God has told him. A commandment, by definition, tells a person to *choose* one of two options.

Had the first commandment been stated as a commandment ("Make Me your God"), it would have implied that the truth of God's existence as the Creator of the world is dependent on the understanding of man. And that is obviously not true.

Thus, our commandment to believe in God is expressed as an unequivocal statement: "I am your God." The deeper meaning of this is that we are *obligated* to see to it that the truth of this statement becomes self-evident; that God's existence is expressed in the world, and that Godly values are incorporated into the fabric of our everyday lives.

Second, the only way that God can command a human being to do something is if that person already believes in Him as God. That understanding must precede any interaction that God can have with humanity.

God, therefore, first stated that He *exists*. Once that was established (by the "statement"), we were obligated to understand our deeper obligation to Him: to make His existence real in the world and in our lives.

The Second Commandment

The second commandment is: "*You must not have any gods of others before Me. You must not make for yourself a sculpture....You must not prostrate yourself to them nor worship them, for I [am] the Eternal, your God..."*

Let us analyze this commandment in depth. The sentence, "*You must not have any gods of others before Me,*" uses two Hebrew words, על פני, "*before Me.*" It could have used the single word לפני (before Me). Why is the word על ("on") used, which seems to denote "Do not have other gods *on* Me"?

The Hebrew word פני (from פנים) has two meanings: (1) face; and (2) inside, or essence. The words *face* and *essence* are related: A person's face (i.e. his expression and eyes), to a sensitive observer, will reflect his essence.

People originally served idols because they believed that man, with all of his limitations and flaws, could not relate to a supernatural God directly. They believed that they could only relate to the physical entities that God created (e.g. the sun and the stars) and the forces of nature (e.g. fertility and growth). Man deduced that he must therefore serve these forces and entities, and not God Himself.

When God says "Do not have other gods על פני" (on פני, on my essence), He is actually saying: "Do not have other gods *on* Me: Do not clothe Me, or conceal me, with the physical entities I have created, and relate to Me through them. Serve Me *directly.*"[19]

* * *

The second commandment lists four things that we must not do:

1. Recognize idols as gods
2. Create idols
3. Prostrate ourselves before idols
4. Worship idols

Why was it necessary for God to give us four *separate* commandments, which basically all tell us one thing: not to have any relationship with idols?

---

19. *Tiferes Yisrael*, chapter 38.

Each prohibition speaks to a different motivating factor for serving idols. Therefore, all four prohibitions were necessary.

There are four possible motivations that may prompt a person to serve idols:

1. He believes that the idol has divine powers.
2. He loves the idol (and desires to serve it).
3. He fears that he will be punished in some way if he does not worship the idol.
4. He has self-interest in serving the idol: e.g. power, social acceptance, or financial benefit.

The first prohibition is "Do not recognize other gods." Here, God speaks to the person who believes in the verity of the idol. Do not recognize them, God says, as being an independent source of power.

The second prohibition is "Do not create images of other gods." A person creates forms of things that he loves; for instance, people take many photographs of their children. Here, God is speaking to a person who is motivated by love.

The third prohibition is "Do not prostrate yourself to them." The term "prostration" is always used to denote worship rooted in fear.[20] Here, God speaks to one who would serve the idol because he is afraid of a physical threat or of punishment if he does not worship it.

The fourth prohibition is "Do not serve them" — לא תעבדם. The term תעבדם comes from the word עבודה, service that is paid for.[21] Here, God speaks to a person who is motivated to serve idols for his own benefit, e.g. a high social status that would come from serving idols, or acceptance by his society.

* * *

---

20. In *Megillas Esther*, for example, when Haman declared himself a deity and forced people to serve him, the megillah says that people prostrated themselves before him.
21. See, for example, *Bereshis* 31:41.

The order in which we are instructed *not* to serve idols is directly parallel to the order in which we *are* encouraged to serve God.

The optimum motivation for serving God is, undoubtedly, a recognition of His existence: We recognize that He is the source of all existence and therefore want to connect to Him.

The next most valid reason for serving God is love. Just as a child loves his parents and wants to fulfill their desires out of love for them, we too can be motivated to do God's will out of our love for Him.

A third level of serving God is fear of punishment for not serving Him. This is a less desirable motivation than the first two, and therefore is counted third.

The least desirable reason to serve God (and do mitzvos) is for personal benefit. Serving God in order to serve oneself is not encouraged. Therefore, it is considered last.[22]

The Third Commandment

The third commandment is: *"You must not swear by the name of the Eternal, your God, in vain, for the Eternal will not absolve him who swears by His name in vain."*

The Talmud[23] states that swearing falsely (especially in God's name) carries a stringency that no other prohibition carries. While the punishment of all sins is delayed to allow the perpetrator to repent, the punishment for this sin is meted out immediately. Let us try to understand why.

Swearing falsely in God's name is not as direct an attack on God as denying His very existence would be. Yet, in some way, it is a more terrible act.

The reason is this: One who denies the existence of God has not really related negatively to God; he has merely cut himself off from God. One who insults God's honor, however, *has* lowered

---

22. *Tiferes Yisrael*, chapter 38.
23. *Shevuos* 39a.

the level of God's honor in the world[24]; a tangible wrongdoing has occurred. This is the only infraction in the Torah that can truly infringe upon God, and that is why it brings a swifter punishment than all the other sins. God exists beyond the limitations of time. The sin, which was perpetrated against God, caused "damage" in a realm that supersedes time. Therefore, the punishment for the sin is also not time-bound: it is immediate.[25]

The Fourth and Fifth Commandments

The fourth commandment orders us to observe the Sabbath, and the fifth commandment instructs us to honor our parents. Indeed, these two mitzvos form a meaningful pair.

The Sabbath day attests that God created the entire world, and expresses God's role as the Creator of the world. However, even something that affirms that God created the world has left one aspect of His authority unconfirmed: While God may have created the universe, who is to say that He relates, specifically, to each individual? Perhaps the great Creator only cares about the great events of the world, and does not have any interest in the trials and tribulations of man on an everyday level? The answer to this question lies in an understanding of the fifth commandment.

The commandment to honor our parents applies equally to a parent who was involved in his child's upbringing and to one who was not. It is not a command to express appreciation for parental involvement in our upbringing; it is appreciation for existence itself. With this commandment, the Torah is telling us that there is a significant relationship between a biological parent and his child (even if the parent is uninvolved in that child's life).

If individual people in the world were unimportant, then the

---

24. As above, God is not affected by any action of mankind. The discussion here is limited to the perspective of man.
25. *Tiferes Yisrael*, chapter 39.

relationship of a biological parent to a child (where there was no involvement in his development) would be random; no obligation would exist to honor the parent. The fact that this obligation does exist tells us that a person's parents are handpicked for him by God, in the context of his unique mission and destiny. There are real reasons why it was specifically his parents who were chosen to be the ones to bring him into the world. This shows that God cares about and relates to each and every individual, just as He relates to and is involved with the world at large.[26]

The Last Five Commandments

The last five commandments relate to man's interpersonal relations. They forbid murder, adultery, theft, false testimony, and jealousy.

The structure of the last five commandments is very different from that of the first five commandments. While each of the first five commandments is followed directly by a rationale for its observance,[27] the last five commandments are not. They say merely: *"You must not murder; You must not commit adultery; You must not steal; You must not give false testimony; You must not desire."* Reasons are not given for them.

Why the difference?

If a statement is made and a reason is given for it, and a second statement is made and a *different* reason is given for it, it is clear that there is no connection between the two statements. For

---

26. *Tiferes Yisrael*, chapter 41.
27. "I am the Eternal, your God — Who took you out of the land of Egypt. You must not have any gods of others before Me — for I, the Eternal, your God, am a zealous God. You must not swear by the Name of the Eternal in vain — for the Eternal will not absolve him who swears by His Name in vain. Remember the Shabbos day — for [in] six days the Eternal made...everything...and He rested on the seventh day. Honor your father and your mother — so that you may live long."

if the two statements were related, one rationale would have sufficed for both!

Individual reasons are given for the first five commandments to show us that they are each independent ideas. Though the order that they follow is surely meaningful, there is no inherent connection between them. A person who violates one of them will not necessarily be led to violate another one of them. (It may cause him to degenerate spiritually, and to sin in a general sense, but not necessarily to transgress one of the other first four commandments.)[28]

Individual reasons are not given for the last five commandments because they *are* inherently connected. They all share the same rationale, and a person who violates one of them will *necessarily* be brought to violate another. One who sins against his fellow will lose his sensitivity towards that person, and eventually do worse things to him. One who is consistently jealous of his fellow will likely end up giving false testimony against him. One who testifies falsely about another person will lose all regard for him, and will be tempted to steal from him — even if he wasn't tempted to steal at first. Stealing possessions from another will lead one to steal even another's wife. And a habitual adulterer will necessarily be led to kill people who stand in his way.

In truth, however, the connection is much deeper: In the physical world there are precise and predictable patterns in the ways that the elements interact. For example, certain chemicals, under given conditions, will trigger specific reactions within the human body.

The Torah says that the spiritual world is no less complex. Certain behaviors create spiritual energies, which necessarily give birth to other spiritual reactions, which will affect future human behavior.

The Torah is telling us that the last five commandments are

---

28. Indeed, while Esav excelled at honoring his father (commandment five), he served idols (violating commandment two).

interconnected, spiritually, in a precise way. One who violates one will violate another. Much as, in the physical world, chemicals react with each other in very precise and predictable ways, in the spiritual world, too, a person's single action will definitely affect his future actions in very specific ways.[29]

---

29. *Tiferes Yisrael*, chapter 42.

8
Torah and Mitzvos

THE TORAH WAS GIVEN to the Jewish People at Mount Sinai over 3300 years ago. Yet, the revelation there was not the first instance of God communicating directly with man. At the beginning of history, God had commanded Adam (and thereby all of humanity) to keep six basic mitzvos.[1] He later gave Noach and his descendants the additional prohibition against eating the limb of a live animal. Avraham, ten generations later, was commanded to circumcise himself and his household. Yaakov, Avraham's grandson, was given the prohibition against eating an animal's sciatic nerve.

Why the Torah Wasn't Given to Avraham

The entire Torah was given to the Jewish People in the year 2448 from Creation, after the Jews had left Egypt and become a nation in their own right. Why wasn't the entire Torah given to either Adam, Avraham, Yitzchak, or Yaakov if each of them could be given individual mitzvos?

Consider this thought. God is eternal. As the word of God, the Torah is an eternal document. The mission that God gave the Jews to spread the message of the Torah is also an eternal mission.

Without doubt, Adam, Avraham, Yitzchak, and Yaakov were people of immense spiritual stature, yet they were individuals.

---

1. They are: The prohibitions against (1) cursing God; (2) idol worship; (3) murder; (4) theft; and (5) sexual immorality; as well as (6) the commandment to set up a court system.

And an individual is limited by his relatively short life span. He can accomplish much, but he cannot accept, nor carry out, an eternal mission. Only a nation can live eternally; only a nation can accept an eternal mission. Thus, it was only after the Jews had left Egypt, and had been transformed into a nation, that an entity existed that could rightfully receive the *eternal* Torah.

The 613 Mitzvos

The Torah outlines the moral framework that God wants the Jewish People to live by. This framework is composed of 248 "positive" mitzvos (things that we are commanded to do) and 365 "negative" mitzvos (things that we are prohibited from doing). Why are the mitzvos, which express God's will, related to the numbers 248 and 365?

The Torah accomplishes two goals. It teaches us how to input positive energy — Godliness and goodness — into the world, through positive actions (the 248 positive mitzvos). And it teaches us how to maintain the existing moral order that God established when He created the world, through the 365 prohibitions, which are intended to keep man from damaging that framework.

There are 248 positive commandments because in all of existence, there is only one entity that can input positive spiritual energy into the world: man. In fact, that is the essence of his purpose on earth: to use every ounce of his strength to affect the world in a positive way. The human body has 248 limbs. Thus, there are 248 ways to input positivity into the world, or 248 active commandments.

Why are there 365 prohibitive commandments?

The sun is the most powerful creation in the universe (vis-à-vis humanity), and can aptly be called the "king of the physical world."[2] The cycle of seasons on earth is created by the

---

2. There are really two "kings" in creation: the sun and man. The sun is the "king" of the general creation (it makes the world run in a uniform cycle), and man is the "king" of each individual creation (he can do with it as he pleases). (*Tiferes Yisrael*, chapter 4)

365-day-long revolution of the sun around the earth. Thus, the number 365 represents the normal functioning of the universe. And therefore, there are 365 ways that one can, but is commanded not to, destroy the basic orderliness of the world. These are the negative commandments.

* * *

There is another way to understand the 365 prohibitive commandments. There are 365 organs in a human body. The number 365 thus represents the normal functioning of the human body. There are 365 potential ways, then, for the body to malfunction. Similarly, the 365 prohibitive commandments prevent us from causing harm to the world.

The combination of the positive and negative commandments comprises the 613 mitzvos of the Torah. The mitzvos are both the safeguard against damage to God's order and the means to bring the world, and ourselves, to completion.[3]

Torah's Covering

The Talmud (*Megillah* 32a) contains this interesting statement: "*Rabbi Parnach said, One who holds a Torah scroll [without its cloth covering], and reads from it, receives no reward for that study.*"

What is the deeper meaning of Rabbi Parnach's words?

Man is composed, essentially, of a metaphysical soul whose source is God. That soul is then "clothed" in a physical body.

The Torah is very similar. It is a metaphysical and sublime entity (the word of God) that should really have no connection to the physical world. However, as the Torah was given to man who exists in the physical world, it was given a physical, tangible expression for man to relate to. Hence, the mitzvos.

---

3. *Tiferes Yisrael*, chapter 5.

Maharal explains that the symbolism cannot be only that "one must serve God with all of his limbs (248), every single day of the year (365)," for if that were the message, there could have been 365 active commandments and 248 prohibitive commandments as well.

The physical action of a mitzvah (e.g. shaking a *lulav* on Sukkos) is a tangible action which "camouflages" the spiritual energy that is the true essence of the mitzvah. When we do mitzvos, then, we are connecting the deepest essence of our souls to the pure, sublime and metaphysical Torah. Somewhere deep inside the enactment of a mitzvah is a bonding of man and Torah. Thus, man and Torah can relate to each other in this world only with their respective "covers" in place.

Traditionally, the Torah scroll is placed in a protective and decorative cloth mantle. This mantle is not just a practical covering, but represents the concept that the Torah must be "clothed" in a physical way, in order for man to connect to it in this world.

Rabbi Parnach is discussing one who holds a Torah scroll without its protective cover. This person clearly lacks an understanding of the incredible holiness of Torah. Because he doesn't understand that Torah requires a cover, he tries to relate to it without one — which is an impossibility. Thus, he has no reward for his study.[4]

Korach and the Rebellion

One year after the Torah was given at Mount Sinai, Korach (Moshe's first cousin) gathered 250 followers and fomented a rebellion against Moshe's authority. "We are all holy people," he argued. "Why should one man, Moshe, rule over us when we are worthy enough to rule ourselves?" (See *Bemidbar* 16:3.)

The Midrash (*Bemidbar Rabbah* 18:1) explains that Korach's motivation for instigating the rebellion was jealousy. He had hoped to be appointed the High Priest, but Aaron, Moshe's brother, had been chosen over him. Korach charged that Moshe appointed Aaron out of deference to his brother. In truth, however, it was God Who had instructed him to do so.

The story culminates with the extraordinary punishment suf-

---

4. *Tiferes Yisrael*, chapter 13.

fered by Korach and his followers. In an unprecedented manner, the earth opened up and literally "swallowed" the entire group. Most dramatically, Korach along with his 250 men, simply *ceased to exist*. Let us try to understand the reason for their unique punishment.

When Korach and his followers challenged Moshe's authority, they denied the truth of the Torah, which explicitly appoints Moshe as the leader of the Jewish People and the transmitter of the Torah. This was not a simple mistake; it challenged the fundamental truth upon which the Torah is based.

The Torah is the word of God, the expression of His will to humanity. God is the only being that exists absolutely, and it is thus He Who establishes the absolute reality upon which the entire world is based. It is His will (or "word") that gives everything else the ability to exist. The Torah is true because it embodies God's will.

In denying Moshe's role as leader of the Jewish People, Korach was denying the word of God. By doing this, Korach and his followers placed themselves, ideologically, in a position diametrically opposed to the Torah. They represented the antithesis of Torah. Therefore, Korach's group simply ceased to exist. Because their ideology defined itself by its denial of the truth of Torah, there was no room, in the reality created by God, for them to exist![5]

Torah Topics

As the Divine word of God, it would seem that the Torah would contain, mostly, discussions about otherworldly, abstract concepts. However, the Torah spends a great deal of time on mundane topics. Laws of honesty in business are discussed; plaintiffs and defendants are spoken of at great length. These are not sublime topics, yet we are assured that their study will bring man closer to God, and will bring him reward in the world to come.

---

5. *Tiferes Yisrael*, chapter 18.

But shouldn't the contemplation of angels, seraphim, and esoteric concepts bring man closer to God and the metaphysical afterlife?

Clearly, the path to eternal reward is the path that leads man to God. The study of grandiose topics and celestial beings may be intellectually fascinating and enlightening, but will not make man more Godlike. Moreover, God's celestial creations, though they are metaphysical, are not really representative of God.

God is True. God is Righteous. And the Torah is the embodiment of God's traits. The study of Torah is thus the pursuit of truth and righteousness in our everyday lives. One who studies Torah, and makes those values an intrinsic part of his being, has indeed come closer to God. Therefore, the only means of our reaching eternal reward lies in the study of Torah, the internalization of its truths, and the integration of its righteousness into our everyday lives.[6]

Torah's Preservative

The Talmud (*Shabbos* 31a) states: "*Torah knowledge is comparable to produce — harvested, stored and bundled away; and yiras Shamayim [the fear of Heaven] is the preservative that keeps the produce from spoiling.*" In other words, theoretically, it is possible for a person to accumulate much Torah knowledge, but never to receive an eternal reward for it. The key to gaining eternal reward is this crucial ingredient, called the fear of God. Why is this so?

Although the study and knowledge of Torah certainly have the potential to bring man to a higher level of being, to a closer connection with God, this is not an automatic process. In order for a person to receive eternal reward, he must have a connection to God, the only force in the world that is eternal.

Man, naturally, is an egocentric being; he has his own needs, desires, and wishes. He naturally is inclined to seek independ-

---

6. *Tiferes Yisrael*, chapter 11.

ence from God, Who places limitations on his personal freedom and places responsibilities upon him.

The fear of God endows life with a *theo*centric focus. A person who fears God, and understands His infinite greatness, does not allow his ego to undo his subservience to God. There is nothing separating him from God, and he is free to connect with Him. He is therefore able to receive reward for his Torah study, as there is no egocentric drive causing a separation between him and God.[7]

Compassionate Mitzvos?

The Torah contains many interpersonal mitzvos that require man to practice compassion towards his fellow human beings. He is enjoined to give charity, visit the sick, and care for the weak. A common perception is that the rationale behind these mitzvos is "God feels compassion for the needy." However, this is an incorrect understanding of the nature of Torah.

In the story of the creation of the world (*Bereshis*, chapter 1), God is referred to by the name *Elokim*, the name that represents His attribute of justice. God originally created this world with the intention of running it according to a strict form of justice: Reward for good deeds and punishment for bad deeds were to have been given out immediately and forcefully. God did not originally intend to employ mercy to run the world. It was introduced

---

7. *Tiferes Yisrael*, chapter 10.

The Talmud gives another example illustrating one who lacks the fear of God: It is like one who has the keys to an inside room, but lacks the keys to the outside door leading into it. Torah study makes man worthy of reaping reward (the inside room), but if he is independent of God (lacking the key to the outside door), he cannot access eternity (*Tiferes Yisrael*, ibid.).

Ahavas Hashem, the love of God, is tremendously powerful, too. Yet, it is only the negation of self, accomplished through *yiras Hashem*, the fear of God, that can bring us to a full connection with God (*Tiferes Yisrael*, ibid.).

later, only because man could not endure in a world based on rigid justice.

The mitzvos, then — even the ones that seem compassionate — predated the introduction of the attribute of mercy to the world. Clearly, these mitzvos transcend a simple "compassionate" rationale.

The mitzvos that God has given us are much, much more than directives for a functioning society and pleasant interaction between people. They are commandments given to man by God for reasons known only to Him, which are rooted in the absolute metaphysical truths upon which this world was created.[8]

Is the Great Number of Mitzvos to Our Benefit?

The Mishnah in *Avos* 4:4 says: "*God desired to benefit the Jews; therefore, He gave them many mitzvos.*" This seems perplexing. How is it that having many mitzvos is to our benefit? On the contrary, one might argue that having fewer mitzvos, fewer obligations, would be much easier, as man would be able to earn reward with less effort.

The Jewish soul is different from the non-Jewish soul. The Jewish soul has within it the ability to be connected to God through the mitzvos, in a way that other souls do not. The more complex Torah is, then, the more comprehensive the potential of the Jewish soul must be. The more multifaceted Torah is, the more prepared the Jewish soul is for a more comprehensive connection to God.[9]

Additionally, the Torah is the means through which the Jewish People purify themselves. The more detailed the Torah is, and

---

8. *Tiferes Yisrael*, chapter 6.

9. Rambam (*Perush Hamishnayos; Avos*) understands this concept differently. He suggests that by having so many mitzvos, every Jew will inevitably fulfill at least one mitzvah fully and correctly; the merit of this mitzvah will earn him the world to come. The Maharal disagrees with this interpretation.

the greater the number of mitzvos it contains, the more levels of purity the Jewish soul is prepared to reach.[10]

Completion

Every human being longs for completion. Every soul yearns for an inner feeling of fulfillment. When one finds his soul mate and gets married, he feels a certain level of completion. When one finds a reliable source of income and is able to support his family comfortably, he also feels a sense of completion.

Yet, the human soul is not easily satisfied. There is always a part of man that is searching for new and deeper levels of fulfillment. What is the source of this longing for completion? And why does it seem to be such a fundamental part of the human condition?

"Completion" is the point where a living thing or an entity can no longer be added to or improved upon. It is the point at which anything added is either superfluous or negative. When God created the world, He made "finished products," entities that were complete in and of themselves. Fish and birds, trees and flowers, were created with all the parts necessary for their survival and the fulfillment of their function in Creation.

Man, however, is different. Man's defining characteristic (that which elevates him above the animal kingdom) is his intelligence — his ability to think, express his thoughts, and apply his thoughts to action. For man to be complete, then, his intelligence

---

10. *Tiferes Yisrael*, chapter 5.

When the Jews said *"we will do and [then] will we hear"* (*Shemos* 24:7) at Sinai, they expressed this too: that their souls were absolutely in consonance with Torah, and as a result they could commit to keeping the Torah even before they heard what it demanded of them.

Interestingly, according to the above-mentioned explanation of the Mishnah, even a Jew who dies without having done mitzvos has still had some spiritual benefit, as his soul, now in the World to Come, is still more "multifaceted" and complex than the soul of a non-Jew (*Tiferes Yisrael*, ibid.)

would have to reach a point where it can no longer be added to. But is this possible? Can man ever reach a point where his understanding and knowledge cannot grow? Seemingly not. How, then, can he ever reach completion?

Through the Torah.

The Torah is the blueprint of all existence. It encompasses all the knowledge and wisdom in the world, and cannot be added to.[11] God gave the Torah to man to learn and internalize. As much as man inculcates the Torah into himself, he will be complete. God gave man the potential for completion just as He gave it to every other thing. But in man, the completion is not inherent; he must find it in, and obtain it from, the Torah.[12]

The Product of the Soul

In creation, we find that many entities produce things attributable only to themselves. For example, the sun produces sunlight, heat, and solar energy. The earth provides the growing ground and the nutrients for vegetation. Water provides basic sustenance for all life.

What product does man create that is attributable only to him?

There are three aspects of man that are capable of production: his body, his speech, and his soul. The products of his body (based on the decisions of his intelligence) are his physical actions and his intellectual achievements. The product of his speech is his

---

11. See *Devarim* 4:2.

12. *Tiferes Yisrael*, chapter 16.

The Midrash (*Koheles Rabbah* 6:6) gives an analogy to illustrate the soul's longing for completion:

A princess marries a simpleton and is continually unhappy. Her husband does not understand why; he has given her the tastiest bowl of porridge in the whole village. But she is unhappy because she knows that there is so much more in the world. So too, the soul can never feel fulfilled from physical acquisitions because it knows of a greater spiritual dimension that is much more fulfilling than anything physical.

communication, in words and in song.

The product of man's soul, his component closest to God, is the mitzvos that he does. Mitzvos are spiritual deeds that regulate man's actions. They are almost always done without personal gain, and reflect the ambitions of man that transcend his physical needs and desires.[13]

---

13. *Tiferes Yisrael*, chapter 1.

9
The Haggadah[1]

ON THE FIRST DAY of Passover we are commanded to eat matzah (unleavened bread). For the remainder of the holiday there is no express commandment to eat matzah, but we are forbidden to eat any leavened bread.

If the symbol of Rosh Hashanah is the shofar, the symbol of Passover is the matzah. The shofar's message for Rosh Hashanah lies in its sound: a piercing, existential cry that awakens our soul's deepest yearning for closeness to God. Whence does matzah draw its significance as the symbol of the festival of freedom?[2]

Matzah

Our first clue to matzah is found in the opening sentence of the Haggadah: "הא לחמא עניא די אכלו אבהתנא בארעא דמצרים" — *This [matzah] is the bread of poverty that our forefathers ate in the land of Egypt.*"

This statement seems to say that matzah commemorates the food that we ate as slaves in Egypt, much as the *maror*, the bitter herbs that we eat, commemorates our bitter suffering there.

---

1. This chapter presents only a taste of Maharal's great commentary on the Haggadah. All references appear in the Haggadah unless otherwise indicated.
2. *Gevuros Hashem*, chapter 51.

The Torah

The Torah, however, presents the matzah in a different light: שבעת ימים תאכל עליו מצות, לחם עוני, כי בחיפזון יצאת מארץ מצרים" — *For seven days you shall eat matzah, a poor man's bread, for in a haste you left Egypt*" (*Devarim* 16:3).

The swiftness of the Exodus reflected its totality. The Torah says that matzah reminds us of the *speed* in which we left Egypt. Our forefathers had prepared dough for the journey out of Egypt, but their transition to freedom happened so quickly that they had to bake it before it leavened. The message of matzah is that, when we left, we made a "clean break" from Egypt, and left no ties to its culture and values.

The Question

Are these two aspects of matzah — poverty, and the haste with which we left Egypt — conciliatory, or are they contradictory?

A Possible Solution

Perhaps we are interpreting the words of the Haggadah incorrectly by emphasizing the wrong words. Perhaps the message of the Haggadah is not *"This is the bread of poverty that our forefathers ate in the land of Egypt,"* but rather, "This is the bread of poverty." The fact that "our forefathers ate [it] in the land of Egypt," is merely an illustration that it is indeed a food eaten by impoverished people.

Freedom

What is the freedom that we celebrate on Passover? Indeed, how is freedom defined? Is it merely the ability to be absolved from all responsibility and restrictions, to be "free" to do whatever we want?

Let us begin by working backwards. What is the opposite of freedom? And what, in the physical world, represents a lack of freedom?

An alloy is an example. A compound that is a blend of two different materials is inherently "unfree." Each component in the new mixture is affected by the qualities of the other, and is unable to express its own pure character.

If an alloy symbolizes the antithesis of freedom, then a pure element expresses freedom. A pure entity that is able to express its qualities unhindered is inherently free.

A poor man stands alone. He has very few belongings to encumber him, to worry him, to take up his time. He is therefore free to focus on his inner self, and to devote his resources to giving expression to his soul's aspirations. This is real freedom.

Matzah is like a poor man. It is a basic bread, made of just flour and water. It is free from yeast, sugar, oil, honey, or any other ingredient that could compromise its basic character and essence. Like a poor man, matzah has nothing that may cause a confusion of essence.

* * *

This concept of freedom from externals being conducive to realizing one's essence is further illustrated by the fact that when God brought the Jewish People out of Egypt to forge an eternal connection with them, He took them into the desert. The intense heat of a desert climate limits life to a great extent. Food does not grow. Commerce is rarely engaged in. Permanent residence is *naturally* discouraged. There are no wars, no peace, no friends, and no enemies. In the desert, there was nothing external to attach itself to the Jewish People, and it was therefore the perfect place for them to forge a connection with God. Free from external concerns, the Jewish *essence* was able to bond with God.[3]

* * *

We can now see how the two aspects of matzah, the "poor man" aspect of matzah found in the Haggadah, and the "haste"

---

[3]. For this reason, during our sojourn in the desert, God provided our food (manna) and clothing (miraculously, our clothes did not wear out).

aspect of matzah found in the Torah, are not mutually exclusive, but rather illustrate the same idea: Matzah symbolizes our freedom from Egypt. The Torah alludes to the quick and total way in which we left Egypt; the Haggadah expresses the fact that when we broke away from Egypt, there was no lingering attachment to their culture. We were a free nation, prepared to connect with God.[4]

* * *

There is another verse that also relates to the bread that we eat on Passover: "זכור את היום הזה אשר יצאתם ממצרים מבית עבדים, כי בחוזק יד הוציא ה' אתכם מזה. ולא יאכל חמץ — *Remember this day that you went out of Egypt, out of the house of slavery, because with a strong hand God took you out of [Egypt]. And leavened bread will not be eaten*" (*Shemos* 13:3).

This verse says that we eat *unleavened* bread to express the *strength* with which God took us out. Is this different from the *speed* with which He took us out, found in *Devarim* 16:3?

Consider: Speed and strength are related concepts. A powerful person is able to act quickly; a weak person is not. A strong person is able to implement his ideas; a weak person is often not. Power and speed are generally found together. Indeed, the message of the two verses is one and the same.

"A Strong Hand and an Outstretched Arm"

ויוציאנו ה' ממצרים ביד חזקה ובזרוע נטויה" — *And God took us out of Egypt with a strong hand and an outstretched arm*" (*Devarim* 26:8).

The above verse refers to the Ten Plagues, which were the means by which God forced the Egyptians to free the Jews. The

---

4. Matzah is eaten in a reclining position (the eating posture of kings) because it expresses freedom. *Maror*, which conversely reminds us of our suffering in Egypt, is eaten in a sitting position.

Interestingly, the Talmud (*Shabbos* 79a) refers to a fresh animal skin, that has not been salted or stretched, as "matzah." Free from any outside influences, the animal skin has the "poor man" quality of matzah.

two terms "a strong hand" and "an outstretched arm" must then refer to two distinct components that are found within the Ten Plagues.

When someone assaults another person, he does so in two stages. First, he hits his opponent, stunning him. Then, he draws his hand back and threatens to strike again. The threat of more blows serves the purpose of wearing down his opponent's will to resist.

Similarly, each of the Ten Plagues came in two stages: (1) its sudden arrival shocked the Egyptians and threw them into a state of confusion; and (2) its continuation for seven days[5] wore down the Egyptians' will to resist. Indeed, this is the deeper meaning of the words of the above verse: "A strong hand" represents the suddenness with which God brought the plague, and "an outstretched arm" represents the wearing down of the Egyptians that took place over the succeeding seven days.[6]

"Had God Not Redeemed Us"

"ואילו לא הוציא הקב"ה את אבותינו ממצרים, הרי אנו ובנינו ובני בנינו משועבדים היינו לפרעה במצרים — *And if the Holy One, Blessed is He, had not taken our forefathers out of Egypt, then we, our children, and our children's children would still be enslaved to Pharaoh in Egypt.*"

This sentence appears perplexing. Could God have not left our forefathers in Egypt, and taken us out at a later time in history? Why is it implied that our freedom today is only possible because our forefathers were freed so long ago?

---

5. See *Shemos* 7:25.
6. *Gevuros Hashem*, chapter 52.
The death of the Egyptian firstborn, the last plague, did not last for seven days, but for a mere moment. What was the "wearing down" aspect in that plague? The Torah recounts that the Egyptians rushed the Jews out of Egypt. Leave now, they said, for if not, we will all be dead (*Shemos* 12:33).
Clearly, the trauma that the last plague generated wore down the Egyptians' will to resist, even though it lasted only a moment.

The basis of the question lies in the focus on the words "our forefathers": Had God not taken *our forefathers* out of Egypt, we would still be slaves today. Perhaps, though, we are to understand it differently, with the focus placed on God: Had *God* not taken our forefathers out of Egypt, we would still be slaves today. The Haggadah is then telling us that only God was able to bring us to freedom. Even the greatest and wisest Jewish leader, or the mightiest and most powerful angel, would not have been able to free our people from slavery in Egypt. Why is this?

The Talmud (*Ta'anis* 2a) makes the following statement: "ג' מפתחות בידו של הקב״ה שלא נמסרו ביד שליח, ואלו הן: מפתח של גשמים ומפתח של חיה ומפתח של תחיית המתים — *There are three keys that God has never entrusted to a messenger: the key to rain, the key to birth, and the key to the resurrection.*"

Every creation in the world has potential, only part of which is realized. For example, a fruit-bearing tree has the potential both to bear fruit and to provide firewood. But it can do only one of these things at any given time: If its ability to bear fruit is "realized," then its ability to yield firewood remains in potential (and vice versa). Similarly, even the atomic bombs harness only a fraction of the energy contained in the atom.

God, however, is completely different. There is no aspect of Him that exists only in potential and is not realized. His essence exists fully at all times. In fact, God is antithetical to the concept of "potential": He is omnipotent because He owns all the power of the world at all times; He is omniscient because He *exists* in all places at the same time.

What can bring an entity from a state of "potential" to a state of "actualization"? Only something that itself is already actualized.

Let us now return to the Talmud's statement.

When a human life is born, it has been brought from potential to actualization. When rainwater, the building block of all life, is created, it has been brought from potential to reality. When our dead bodies will live again at the time of redemption, they will have been brought from potential to actuality.

That is why it is fitting for God alone to maintain these three "keys" at all times. It is thus fitting for the One Who epitomizes actualization — God Himself — to bring these things into existence.

* * *

The Exodus from Egypt marked our transformation from a group of people, with the *potential* to become a nation, into a nation. It was our people's birth process. And as only God can actualize birth, it follows that had *God* not freed our forefathers, we would have been slaves today; our potential to become a nation would not have been realized.[7]

"Had We All Been Wise"

"ואפילו כולנו חכמים, כולנו נבונים, כולנו זקנים, כולנו יודעים את התורה, מצוה עלינו לספר ביציאת מצרים — *And even if we would all be wise, understanding, sagacious, and learned in Torah, it would still be a mitzvah for us to tell about the Exodus from Egypt.*"

Four terms are used here to denote different aspects of our intelligence: wisdom; understanding; sagaciousness; and Torah knowledge. These four terms are meant to encompass everything that we know.[8]

Wisdom refers to things that we understand conceptually. We know that a whole is larger than a half, and that hot and cold cannot exist in the same place simultaneously. The more one understands conceptually, the wiser he is.

Understanding refers to the deductions that we make based on the things we know. We understand that if a whole is larger than

---

7. *Gevuros Hashem*, chapter 52.
8. There is another very basic level of knowledge that is not included in these four levels: *simple observation* (e.g. we know that fire burns and that trees grow leaves). This aspect of knowledge is not mentioned because the Haggadah is focusing on *human* comprehension. Simple observation is in the domain of animals as well.

a half, then a half is larger than a quarter. We understand that if fire is hot, then coals, which are aglow but are not aflame, are not as hot as fire. The more one can deduce from the things he already knows, the more understanding he has.

Sagaciousness refers to the insights acquired through our life experiences. When to take a stand on an issue, and when to remain silent; when to join the masses, and when to stand alone. The more one learns from his life experiences, the more sagacious he is.

Torah knowledge refers to information that we have been taught. Most of the information that we know, we have heard from others. News items are based on other people's testimony. Historical fact is based on the research of scholars. Similarly, our understanding of the Torah comes from the understanding of our parents and teachers, who have been taught by their parents and teachers, in a chain all the way back to Sinai. The more information one has been taught, the more he is "a knower of the Torah."

Thus, the Haggadah is telling us that even one who excels in all four areas of knowledge — and who understands the Exodus in all of these four dimensions — has an obligation to retell the story of the Exodus at his Seder.[9]

"I Took You Out"

ויוציאנו: לא על ידי מלאך, לא על ידי שרף, ולא על ידי שליח, אלא הקב"ה בכבודו ובעצמו — *God took us out [of Egypt]* (*Devarim* 26:8): *Not by means of a (good) angel, and not by means of a fiery (destructive) angel, and not by means of a messenger. Rather, it was the Holy One in His Glory, by Himself!"*

Technically, there were three possible ways for God to have taken us out of Egypt:

1. He could have sent a (good) angel to lead us out of slavery;
2. He could have sent a destructive angel to destroy the

---

9. *Gevuros Hashem*, chapter 52.

Egyptians, thereby enabling us to flee Egypt; or
3. He could have freed us in a natural way. Empires rise and fall over the centuries, and Egyptian civilization could have been overtaken militarily by a society that believed slavery was immoral. This people could have then freed us.

The point of the *midrash* is that God rejected each one of these possibilities:

1. He did not send a (good) angel, i.e. the angel Michael who enacts positive missions.[10]
2. He did not send a fiery, destructive angel to free us by destroying the Egyptians, i.e. the angel Gavriel who enacts destructive missions.[11]
3. He did not send a messenger, i.e. His great messenger, nature[12] (the natural flow of history), to free us.[13] He chose to free us Himself!

How God Took Us Out

ויוציאנו ה' ממצרים ביד חזקה, ובזרוע נטויה, ובמורא גדול, ובאותות ובמופתים"

— *God took us out of Egypt with a strong hand, an outstretched arm,*

---

10. Of the three angels who visited Avraham in *Parashas Vayeira*, it was Michael's mission to save Lot. Not coincidentally, the word מלאך (angel), and the word מכאל, Michael, are made up of the same letters.

11. Of the angels who visited Avraham, it was Gavriel's mission to destroy Sdom. Similarly, God sent the angel Gavriel to destroy the camp of Ashur and save the Jews (see *Divrei Hayamim* II 32:21).

12. Nature is the quintessential messenger, as it does exactly what God commands it to do. It has no will, does not seek to change itself, and merely perpetuates the cycles established by God.

13. *Gevuros Hashem*, chapter 55.

Consider another reason that God took the Jewish People out of Egypt Himself: He did it in order to bring them to Sinai to forge an intimate connection with them. Is it not logical that God wished to start that very connection by taking us out of Egypt without an intermediary?

with great trepidation, signs, and wonders" (*Devarim* 26:8).

This verse uses five different terms to describe how God took us out of Egypt. Since the Ten Plagues were the instrument of God used to effect our freedom, these terms must describe the plagues in their totality.

The Midrash elaborates: ביד חזקה: זו הדבר, בזרוע נטויה: זו החרב, במורא גדול: זו גילוי שכינה, באותות: זה המטה, ובמופתים: זה הדם — *With a strong hand: This refers to the pestilence; With an outstretched arm: This refers to [God's] sword; With great awe: This refers to the revelation of the Shechinah [Divine Presence]; With signs: This refers to [Moshe's] staff; With wonders: This is the blood* (*Haggadah*).

If we analyze the plagues, we find that they had two goals: to punish the Egyptians, and to teach them (and all of humanity) that God controls the world. The first three terms in our verse refer to the first purpose of the Ten Plagues, and the last two terms refer to the second purpose.

To Punish the Egyptians

God punished the Egyptians in three ways:
1. By withholding their basic necessities (food and water) — (an "indirect" punishment)
2. By smiting them bodily (a "direct" punishment)
3. By revealing Himself to the Egyptians and frightening them, thereby incapacitating them (a punishment containing both direct and indirect elements).[14]

The first three terms in the verse correspond to the three parts of the punishment that God meted out to the Egyptians:
1. *With a strong hand: This is the pestilence.* The plague of pestilence decimated the Egyptian livestock, wiping away a

---

14. God's revelation did not hurt the Egyptians *per se*; it was rather their terrified reaction to His revelation that hurt them.

As we have mentioned previously concerning other Torah themes, the third entity expresses a synthesis of the first two entities.

major source of Egypt's food. As devastating as it was, however, this was an indirect punishment.

2. *With an outstretched arm: This is [God's] sword.* The "sword" refers to the plagues that God brought directly onto the bodies of the Egyptians: the plagues of frogs, lice, wild animals, boils, hail, and the death of the firstborn. Just as a sword directly strikes its target (as opposed to an arrow, which is shot from afar), God punished the Egyptians directly.

3. *With great trepidation: This is the revelation of the Divine Presence.* Beginning with the third plague (see *Shemos* 8:15), the Egyptians were forced to admit that the plagues were the work of God. They were terrified and intimidated by the revelation of God's existence; the fear was physically painful.[15]

To Show God's Control over the World

The second goal of the Ten Plagues was to demonstrate God's control over the world. The last two items mentioned in the verse refer to this accomplishment.

If one wants to show that he can control and manipulate a mechanism, he can either work with its existing structure and make adjustments to it, or he can change it entirely. In these two ways, God showed his control over the greatest "mechanism" in the world — nature itself.

1. *With signs: This is [Moshe's] staff.* A "sign" is an act that shows God's control over the world by working within nature's existing patterns. Most of the plagues exaggerated nature, e.g. the plagues of frogs and lice were merely vast, albeit abnormal multiplications of existing species. The staff of Moshe was used to bring these plagues,[16] and

---

15. This pain was independent of the actual harm they suffered as a result of the plagues.

16. See *Shemos* 8:1, 8:12.

therefore captures this concept.

2. *With wonders: This is the blood.* The only plague that totally changed nature was the plague of blood. It was indeed wondrous that water was transformed into blood. And that is why the "wonders" in this *midrash* refer to the plague of blood.

* * *

In the aforementioned elaboration, the first three terms in our verse refer to the first purpose of the Ten Plagues (punishing the Egyptians), and the last two terms refer to their second purpose (the demonstration of God's control over the world). However, it is possible to explain all five terms as references to the second idea — that of showing God's control over the world. The breakdown in this explanation would be as follows: The first three terms express God's control over the *natural* world, and the last two express God's control over the *miraculous* world.

Consider:

There are three dimensions in the physical world, and in mankind:

1. The *chomer* (raw materials, e.g. wood, stone, and clay; in man, the human body);
2. The *tzurah* (that which gives shape to the raw materials; e.g. a mold, a form; in man, the soul); and
3. The composites of *chomer* and *tzurah* (the "functioning" entities that exist, e.g. a table, a chair; in man, a human being. A human being is an entity whose *chomer* and *tzurah* work in concert and coexist harmoniously).

The first three terms mentioned in the verse refer to God showing His control over these three aspects of creation.

1. *With a strong hand*: This is the pestilence. In the plague of pestilence, the Egyptians' animals died. By destroying the raw material of the Egyptians, God showed that He controlled all of the *chomer* in the world.

2. *With an outstretched arm*: This is [God's] sword. This term (as in the previous explanation) refers to those plagues which harmed the Egyptians bodily, directly. A sword, which strikes its target directly, is used to break down edifices and people. In acting directly upon the Egyptian character and people, God expressed His control over the *tzurah* aspect of creation.
3. *With great trepidation*: This is the revelation of the Divine Presence.

The Ten Plagues were a composite of the physical and the spiritual: They were physical phenomena, yet their essence was spiritual, as they were a dramatic revelation of God's presence. This demonstrated God's control over the composite of *chomer* and *tzurah*, the physical and the spiritual.

The last two terms mentioned, signs and wonders, as in the first explanation, express God's control over the realm of the miraculous: Signs symbolize God's ability to exaggerate or adjust the phenomena in the physical world, and wonders symbolize God's ability to change the physical world.[17]

The Ten Statements and the Ten Plagues

The opening chapter of *Bereshis* tells us that the world was created in six days. However, the Mishnah in *Avos* (5:1) explains that God used ten "statements" to bring the world into existence.

The words "God said" are found nine times in the story of creation in *Bereshis*, and the words "In the beginning [God created]" also constitute a statement.[18]

---

17. *Gevuros Hashem*, chapter 56.

18. The reason that the first statement is worded differently from the other statements may be because whereas the first statement created something from nothing (*ex nihilo*), the other statements formed new entities from material that had already existed (e.g. fish developed from the water, animals and man were formed from the ground).

These are the Ten Statements:
1. *"In the beginning [God created]"* (*Bereshis* 1:1).
2. *"God said: 'The waters shall produce swarms of low-creeping living creatures'"* (*Bereshis* 1:20).
3. *"God said: 'The waters below the heavens shall be concentrated into one place, and the dry ground will [thus] become visible'"* (*Bereshis* 1:9).
4. *"God said: 'The earth shall produce living creatures'"* (*Bereshis* 1:24).
5. *"God said: '[The] luminaries shall be [positioned] in the sky'"* (*Bereshis* 1:14).
6. *"God said: 'Let us form man with our mold'"*(*Bereshis* 1:26).
7. *"God said: 'The firmament shall [form] between the waters, and it shall separate between [the lower] waters and [the upper] waters'"* (*Bereshis* 1:6).
8. *"God said: 'The land shall...[produce] trees of fruit that produce fruit'"* (*Bereshis* 1:11).
9. *"God said: 'There shall be light'"* (*Bereshis* 1:3).
10. *"God said: 'I have hereby given you every plant...and all trees...to eat'"* (*Bereshis* 1:29).

In the Torah, we find that many similar concepts are intrinsically related. The number ten is associated both with the creation of the world and with the Ten Plagues. What is the deeper connection between the two?

As mentioned above, one of the purposes of the Ten Plagues was to show that God controlled the world in its every facet. With each plague, God manipulated a different part of creation, which had come about through one of the Ten Statements of Creation. Let us see how the Ten Plagues correspond to the Ten Statements of Creation.

1. The plague of blood corresponds to the statement, *"God said: 'I have hereby given you every plant...and all trees...to eat.'"*[19]

The body is sustained by food, whose nutrients are incorporated into the bloodstream. By turning Egypt's water into blood, God expressed His control over the sustenance of Mankind.

2. The plague of frogs corresponds to the statement, "*God said: 'The waters shall produce swarms of low-creeping living creatures.'*"

With the plague of frogs, God showed His control over the lowly creeping creatures of the world.

3. The plague of lice corresponds to the statement, "*God said: 'The waters below the heavens shall be concentrated into one place, and the dry ground will [thus] become visible.'*"

In this plague, God showed His control over the earth, which spawned the lice that inundated Egypt.

4. The plague of wild animals corresponds to the statement, "*God said: 'The earth shall produce living creatures.'*"

With the masses of wild animals that descended upon Egypt, God demonstrated His control over the animal kingdom.

5. The plague of pestilence corresponds to the statement, "*God said: '[The] luminaries shall be [positioned] in the sky.'*"

The Midrash teaches that the stars, through their positions in the sky, tell of events that have not yet occurred on earth.[20]

The plagues of pestilence brought death to many animals; it

---

19. The first plague expressed God's control over the last act of creation, and (as we will soon see) the last plague demonstrated God's control over the first act of creation.

At first, God wished to display only a minimal part of His control of the world; He therefore only manipulated His last act of creation. Had that been enough to convince the Egyptians to free the Jews, He would not have revealed Himself more. However, the Egyptians did not free the Jews, and ultimately, God was forced to bring the most devastating tenth plague, which undid the first, and most substantial, act of creation. (Maharal bases this point on the order of the first and last plagues; the other plagues follow no specific order.)

20. See *Shemos Rabbah* 1:22.

was an occurrence of great proportion. It was thus preceded by a change in the positioning of the stars. It follows, then, that God's changing the position of the stars showed that he controlled them.

6. The plague of boils corresponds to the statement, "*God said: 'Let us form man with our mold.'*"

The boils disfigured the bodies of the Egyptians. By causing a deformity in man, God expressed that it was He who had formed him to begin with.

7. The plague of hail corresponds to the statement, "*God said: 'The firmament shall [form] between the waters, and it shall separate between [the lower] waters and [the upper] waters.'*"

The hail was created high above the earth (in the clouds). God expressed His control over the separation between the upper and lower waters by removing that separation for a moment, and allowing hail to fall onto the earth.

8. The plague of locusts corresponds to the statement, "*God said: 'The land shall...[produce] trees of fruit that produce fruit.'*"

While other plagues also destroyed crops (e.g. hail), only the plague of locusts was specifically directed at the vegetation. Through this plague, God showed His control over the plant kingdom.

9. The plague of darkness corresponds to the statement, "*God said: 'There shall be light.'*"

By extending darkness to the daytime, and eliminating normal daylight, God exhibited His control over light.

10. The death of the Egyptian firstborn corresponds to the statement, "*In the beginning [God created].*"

The firstborn represents the beginning. By destroying the Egyptian firstborn, God expressed that it was He Who had created all "firsts"; it was He Who created the universe, *ex nihilo*.[21]

---

21. *Gevuros Hashem*, chapter 57.

"How Many Favors"

In the portion of the Haggadah called *Kama Ma'alos Tovos*/How Many Favors (commonly called *Dayeinu*), we thank God for fifteen blessings that He bestowed upon our people, from the time of our Exodus until the building of our Holy Temple.

> How many favors God bestowed on us.... He took us out of Egypt; He wrought judgments upon [the Egyptians]; [He destroyed] their gods; He slew their firstborn; He gave us their wealth; He split the sea for us; He took us through [the sea] on dry land; He drowned our enemies in [the sea]; He gave us our needs in the desert for forty years; He gave us manna to eat; He gave us the Shabbos; He brought us to Mount Sinai; He gave us the Torah; He brought us to the Land of Israel; He built us the Temple.

These fifteen expressions of praise can be broken down into three sets of five.

> How many favors God bestowed on us!
> 1. He took us out of Egypt.
> 2. He wrought judgments upon [the Egyptians].
> 3. [He destroyed] their gods.
> 4. He slew their firstborn.
> 5. He gave us their wealth.
> 6. He split the sea for us.
> 7. He took us through [the sea] on dry land.
> 8. He drowned our enemies in [the sea].
> 9. He gave us our needs in the desert for forty years.
> 10. He gave us manna to eat.
> 11. He gave us the Shabbos.
> 12. He brought us to Mount Sinai.
> 13. He gave us the Torah.
> 14. He brought us to the Land of Israel.
> 15. He built us the Temple.

The first set of five express thanks for our Exodus from Egypt, which resulted in the birth of our nation. The second set of five thank God, not only for forming us as a people, but also for suspending nature and performing miracles on our behalf during and after the Exodus. The third set of five thank God not only for doing miracles for us, but also for forging an eternal bond with us.

Let us now observe the sequence of the praises *within* each set of five.

Exodus

1. *He took us out of Egypt.*

We begin by thanking God for the most basic, elemental aspect of our freedom.

2. *He wrought judgments upon [the Egyptians].*

We then note that in addition to freeing us, God avenged us and punished our tormentors.

3. *[He destroyed] their gods.*

We then add that in addition to smiting the Egyptians, God destroyed their gods. The devastation of the Egyptian value system was even more significant than their physical military defeat.

4. *He slew their firstborn.*

We further mention that in addition to destroying their gods, God killed the Egyptians' firstborn sons. The firstborn of Egypt represented the core of its people. Without their essence intact, the Egyptians would not be able to rebuild their society.

5. *He gave us their wealth.*

We then observe that besides decimating our enemies, God did us the extra favor of transferring to us their wealth. This warrants added thanks.

Miracles

6. *He split the sea for us.*

We begin by thanking God for the miracles that He did for us, beginning with the splitting of the Red Sea.

7. *He took us through [the sea] on dry land.*

We then note that in addition to actually splitting the sea, God also made the seafloor completely dry, so we could walk through it comfortably, unimpeded by mud. We would have been just as happy to cross the Red Sea on muddy ground; God, in His great love for us, performed this added miracle for our benefit.

8. *He drowned our enemies in [the sea].*

We then add that in addition to taking us out of Egypt in a comfortable manner, God also drowned the Egyptians. Technically, this did not have to happen; the Egyptians could have been forced back into Egypt without being killed.

9. *He gave us our needs in the desert for forty years.*

We then recognize that in addition to performing miracles for us when we left Egypt, God miraculously provided for all of our physical needs, for the entire forty years we spent in the desert.

10. *He gave us the manna to eat.*

We then add that in addition to taking care of our general needs, God also created a special food for us. Manna was the greatest miracle of all, as it represented not just the suspension or manipulation of nature, but the creation of something supernatural.

Our Connection to God

11. *He gave us the Shabbos.*

We begin by thanking God for giving us Shabbos, an eternal covenant, a special gift that binds us to Him.[22]

---

22. *Shemos* 31:16.

12. *He brought us to Mount Sinai.*

We then add that, besides giving us Shabbos, God also brought us to Mount Sinai. While Shabbos represented the Divine covenant, Sinai brought us a connection to God's Presence itself, even without the Torah.

13. *He gave us the Torah.*

We then note that in addition to bringing us to Sinai, God gave us the Torah. Although Sinai forged a connection between us and God through our five *senses* (which *perceived* His revelation), it was only for the duration of the revelation. The Torah, however, allows us to connect to God through our *minds*, and on a continual basis.

14. *He brought us to the Land of Israel.*

We then mention that in addition to giving us the Torah, God gave us the exalted Land of Israel. The Talmud[23] says: "One who lives outside the Land of Israel [is like one who] has no God." This teaches us that one who gives up the opportunity to live in the Land of Israel has a much weaker connection to God than one who does reside there. Living in the Land of Israel enables one to be especially close to God.

15. *He built us the Temple.*

In our final expression of praise, we thank God for the Temple, the ultimate means of connecting with Him. The most direct path to a relationship with God is via the Temple, where the Divine Presence rests and is apparent to all, and where a person can be inspired to connect to God in a very strong way.[24]

The Pascal Offering (Korban Pesach)

I will pass through the land of Egypt...and strike down every firstborn.... The blood [of the Pascal offering] will act for you as a

---

23. *Kesuvos* 110b.
24. *Gevuros Hashem*, chapter 59.

*sign on the houses...I shall see the blood and skip over you....
This day [every year] shall be...a remembrance [of that miracle],
and you shall celebrate it as a festival* (cf. *Shemos* 12:12–14).

On the night immediately preceding the Exodus, God brought the final plague upon the Egyptians — the plague of the Firstborn. The Jews were commanded to take blood from the Pascal offering brought that day, and spread it on their doorposts. This blood would serve as a "sign" for God to skip over their houses, as He descended on Egypt to take the life of every firstborn male.

Interestingly, in the preceding nine plagues there was nothing that externally differentiated the Jews from the Egyptians. Nonetheless, the Jews were not affected by the plagues. For example, the Midrash tells us that during the plague of blood, if a Jew and an Egyptian sipped from a cup simultaneously, the Jew would draw water and the Egyptian would draw blood.[25] Why was a special protection needed for the last plague?

There is a significant difference between the first nine plagues and the last plague: While the first nine plagues were enacted by angels carrying out God's will, the last plague was done by God Himself.

Because the first nine plagues were carried out by angels — whose powers are limited by their specific instructions from God — they were only able to affect their intended object, the Egyptians, and not the Jews. The last plague, however, was carried out by God, Who is both omniscient and omnipotent. What would prevent the plague of the firstborn from harming the Jews?

God therefore instructed the Jewish People to bring the Pascal offering. The Pascal offering brought about an intimate connection between the Jewish People and God.[26] The spreading

---

25. *Shemos Rabbah* 9:9.

26. God instructed us to bring the Pascal offering because in some metaphysical way it effected an unequaled unity between the Jewish People and Himself.

of blood on their doorposts signified that connection. Once the Jews were connected to God, they were safe; for — consider — just as God could not be affected by the plague He brought, neither could they.

Overwhelmingly, the laws of the Pascal offering reflect a nature of connection and oneness:

- The Pascal offering is a sheep, an animal symbolic of unity. The Midrash says: "Why are the Jewish People compared to a sheep? [Because] just as a sheep, when one of its limbs is hurt, feels the pain throughout its entire body, so too the Jews. Even if only one Jew sins, all the Jews will be punished."[27]
- The sheep must be perfect and unblemished. Wholeness expresses unity as no part of the entity is missing. We can also see this in Torah, where the completion of the Tabernacle (*Shemos* 36:13) is expressed by the words, "And the Tabernacle was one."
- The Pascal offering must be male. Conceptually, the male is the *tzurah* of creation, who organizes disparate *chomer* into a unified form.
- The sheep must be roasted. Roasted meat becomes dry; it loses water as its volume contracts. As it contracts, its fibers draw closer together — an expression of unity. This is in contrast to cooked meat, which softens, and often breaks into pieces.
- The Pascal offering is the only *korban* that is roasted whole; no other offering is prepared in that way.
- The Torah adds a special verse prohibiting the cooking of the Pascal offering. Indeed water is the quintessential *chomer* — as it has no form and takes on the shape of the container it is in — and thus, water has no place near the

---

27. *Vayikra Rabbah* 4:6, regarding the story of Achan. Only Achan sinned, but all the Jews were chastised for it. (See *Yehoshua*, chapter 7.)

Pascal offering.

⋄ When the Pascal meat is eaten, none of its bones may be broken; they must remain whole.

⋄ The Pascal offering must be eaten by family and friends together in one house. It may not be divided up among friends to eat separately in their own homes. This too is an expression of unity.

⋄ The Pascal offering must be one (complete) year old.[28]

Pesach, Matzah, U'maror

ואכלו את הבשר בלילה הזה צלי אש, ומצות מרורים יאכלוהו" — *They shall eat [the Pascal offering together] with matzos…[and] maror"* (*Shemos* 12:8).

On Passover night, we are commanded to eat the Pascal offering together with matzah and *maror*. What is the significance of eating these things together?

The answer to this question lies in the fact that, as mentioned above, the Pascal offering relates to the oneness of the Jewish People with God, and, ultimately, the Oneness of God. (The only reason that the Jewish People can truly become one with God is because God is One. It is impossible to become one with a fractured entity.)

Regarding monotheism, there is an argument that some heretics present: "How can a single God create contradictory forms of existence: light and darkness, heat and cold?"

The Torah addresses this question by commanding us to eat the Pascal offering together with matzah and *maror*.

Matzah is a symbol of freedom; *maror* is a symbol of slavery. They represent polar opposites. By eating the Pascal offering (which expresses God's Unity), together with matzah and *maror* (which express contradictory concepts), we are expressing the *meaning* of the Unity of God. What is the meaning of God's Unity?

---

28. *Gevuros Hashem*, chapter 60.

It is that God encompasses everything; that there is nothing that exists independently of God. As nothing exists independent of God, everything that does exist, must exist within Him. God is One simply because there is nothing else. And if God is One, even contradictory entities are His creations as well.

* * *

There is an additional reason for eating the Pascal offering together with matzah and *maror*.

When we say that God is One and controls the whole world, we say that He controls all of the spectra found in nature.

The extremes of a paradigm express its entirety. For example, "freedom" and "slavery" express the entire paradigm of "personal status." We express God's full control over the "personal status" paradigm by eating the Pascal offering, which represents the Oneness of God, with matzah and *maror*, each of which represents one extreme of this paradigm. Eating these three foods together not only demonstrates that God controls both of these extremes and this entire paradigm, but also that He controls every other paradigm that exists as well.

The connection of *Pesach* (the Pascal offering), matzah, and *maror* carries another message, too, relating to the deeper meaning of the Jews' unique connection to God. The Talmud (*Shabbos* 156a) says that while all the nations of the world have a *sar* (a heavenly representative that both protects it and advocates on its behalf before God), the Jewish People do not. Their close relationship with God does not allow for an intermediary to exist between them.

Thus, when the Jews are connected to God and His Torah, no one can do them harm. They are nourished by God and need nothing from any other nation. But when they stop doing God's will and are distanced from God, then they are inevitably worse off than any other nation — not having a *sar* watch over them, they are entirely unprotected.

Matzah is the symbol of freedom; *maror* is the symbol of slavery. They are eaten with the *Pesach* offering to express our special relationship with God. Our history is filled with grandeur and servitude, because of the *Pesach* offering which represents our special unity with God.[29]

The Four Cups

ד' כוסות הם נגד הד' לשונות של גאולה, שנאמר: והוצאתי...והצלתי...וגאלתי... ולקחתי (*Shemos Rabbah* 6:4).

When God took the Jews out of Egypt, they experienced four levels of freedom. These levels are paralleled by four "expressions of freedom" used in the Torah; these expressions are represented by the four cups of wine we drink at the Pesach Seder. The "expressions of freedom" are God's statements which defined our freedom: (1) *"I will remove you from the burdens of Egypt"* (והוצאתי); (2) *"I will save you from your work"* (והצלתי); (3) *"I will redeem you"* (וגאלתי); and (4) *"I will take you to Me as a nation"* (ולקחתי).

Let us begin by explaining the first three.

Long before our actual enslavement, the blueprint of our slavery in Egypt was predicted when God spoke to Avraham at the *Bris bein Habesarim*.

At the *Bris bein Habesarim*, God told Avraham: "כי גר יהיה זרעך בארץ לא להם, ועבדום, ועינו אותם — *Your descendants will be foreigners in a land that is not theirs, [the inhabitants] will enslave them, and they will oppress them"* (*Bereshis* 15:13).

The prophecy foretold three separate things: The Jews would (1) be foreigners in a strange land; (2) be enslaved there; and (3) be oppressed by their host nation. Indeed, these are all separate hardships, as one can be a foreigner without being enslaved, and can be enslaved without being seriously afflicted.

In the Exodus from Egypt, God reversed these three levels of suffering, beginning with the most difficult one.

The first expression, *"I will remove you from the burdens of Egypt,"* refers to the removal of the *oppression* that caused us so

---

29. *Gevuros Hashem*, chapter 60.

much suffering. The word "burdens" denotes severe affliction. We thank God for removing our affliction with the first cup of wine.

The second expression, "*I will save you from your work*," refers to our freedom from enslavement. "Work" denotes slave labor (and not necessarily affliction). The second cup of wine represents thanks for this level of freedom.

The third expression, "*I will redeem you*," alludes to the fact that God removed our detrimental alien status. In redeeming us, God removed the feelings of insecurity and isolation that are part and parcel of being strangers in another's land. The third cup expresses thanks for this.

Once these three levels of freedom were accomplished, God then moved to bring us to a new level: He made us His chosen nation. The fourth expression of freedom, "*I will take you to Me as a nation*," is the most glorious of all. God did much more than free our bodies from servitude. He chose us to be His beloved chosen nation and forged an eternal bond with us. The fourth cup of wine thanks God for this.

* * *

There is another explanation of the four expressions of freedom.

The first two expressions reflect the two (natural) reasons that our people were enslaved:

1. The Jews were a growing threat to Egyptian society. They were prosperous and successful, and professed a moral code much higher than Egypt's. Their numbers were also growing rapidly, which posed a potential military threat. Therefore, Pharaoh enslaved them in order to avoid future challenges.
2. Pharaoh himself was an evil person. He would do anything for his personal gain, and morality meant nothing to him. In fact, the Midrash[30] tells us that Pharaoh even

---

30. *Shemos Rabbah* 6:5.

slaughtered innocent children in a demented attempt to improve his health. Thus, even if the Jews were not a military threat, they were susceptible to enslavement because their slave labor would benefit Pharaoh personally.

The expression *"I will remove you from the burdens of Egypt"* refers to the freedom from burdens that were inherent in the Jews' experience as foreigners in the land of Egypt. The simple fact that they were a growing minority made them susceptible to enslavement by the majority. This expression of freedom refers to God's freeing us from our predisposition to enslavement.

The expression *"I will save you from your work"* uses the Hebrew word *hitzalti*/saved. The word *hatzal* is always used in reference to saving something from an *external* threat or danger. Thus, it refers to God's saving us from the cruelty of Pharaoh, which was based on nothing else but Pharaoh's personal depravity.[31]

The last two expressions of freedom, as in our previous explanation, define the levels of freedom that God gave us.

The third expression of freedom, *"I will redeem you,"* says that God gave us the benefit of not feeling like strangers in a foreign land.

The fourth expression, *"I will take you to Me as a nation,"* says that God not only freed us from slavery, but also brought us close to Him.

Matzah vs. Wine

As mentioned above, matzah represents freedom. Yet, we mark the four expressions of freedom with wine. Why not with matzah?

Indeed, there is a difference between matzah and wine.

The Gemara[32] says: "יין נתן בע' וסוד נתן בע'" — Wine is given with seventy, and secrets are given with seventy." Both the

---

31. *Gevuros Hashem*, chapter 60.
32. *Eruvin* 65a.

words יין — wine and סוד — secret have a *gematria* of seventy. This reflects a deep connection between them. Wine is a "secret," as it is not visible on its source, the grapevine. It only emerges later, after a long process of extraction and development. Similarly, a person's secrets are close to his essence, and they are not easily revealed.

A vine, unlike most other plants, cannot be grafted with another tree. Its essence always remains pure, unsullied and untainted by foreign substances. So too, a person's essence can never be captured or controlled by a foreign entity.

It is fitting, then, that wine, the fruit of the vine, has the power to loosen the tongue and reveals a person's secrets, which are expressions of his deepest essence.

Wine is no ordinary beverage, as it touches the core of man. Matzah, in contrast, is merely a mundane food, necessary for basic sustenance and the survival of mankind, and possesses no lofty qualities. Thus, matzah is used to celebrate our *physical* Exodus from Egypt, our basic transition from slavery to freedom. Wine, however, is used to celebrate the loftier aspects of freedom: the changes in our personal experience, which ultimately results in a bond with God — alluded to in the four expressions of freedom.[33]

The Connection between the Third and Fourth Cups

The third cup of wine represents "*I will redeem you*" (freedom), and the fourth cup represents "*I will take you to Me as a nation*" (chosenness). A number of Halachic laws say that there is to be a connection between them.

- ◇ One may not eat or drink anything between the third and the fourth cups of wine.
- ◇ The third paragraph in the tefillin parchment (which includes "*I will redeem you*") is attached, without spaces, to

---

33. *Gevuros Hashem*, chapter 60.

the fourth paragraph (which includes "*I will take you to Me*").

◊ During the *Shacharis* prayer each morning, one is prohibited from interrupting between the words גאל ישראל/The redeemer of Israel and the *Amidah* (main prayer); the expression of freedom must lead to a connection with God.

This connection between redemption and chosenness is significant indeed, as it defines our freedom. Freedom is not just the ability to do whatever one wants. Freedom means being free from the distractions that pull at us that camouflage the yearning of our souls. Freedom is being able to connect with the Source of our souls: God. Thus, freedom — "*I will redeem you*" — must be connected very strongly to God — "*I will take you to Me as a nation.*" Freedom is celebrated only inasmuch as it leads us to a relationship with God.

This same concept is found regarding the Omer offering. On the second day of Passover (the celebration of our freedom), we begin counting the forty-nine days to Shavuos (the celebration of our receiving the Torah). The message of the counting is that our exodus from slavery in Egypt is significant only because it leads us to a deeper connection with God.

Thus, just after Pesach begins, we look forward to Shavuos, to give our freedom meaning, to give it a Divine purpose.[34]

---

34. *Gevuros Hashem*, chapter 60.

10
Maharal on Hallel[1]

Hallelukah! Give praise, O servants of the Lord from this time forth and for ever more. From the rising of the sun to its setting, the Lord's name is to be praised. The Lord is high above all the nations, and His glory is above the heavens. Who is like the Lord our God, Who is enthroned on high and yet looks far down to behold the things that are in heaven and on the earth?

He raises the needy from the dust, from the trash heaps He raises the destitute, to seat them with the nobles, the nobles of His people. He transforms the barren woman into a joyful mother of children. Hallelukah!

Let us decipher the opening paragraph of *Hallel* (*Tehillim* 113). King David begins by proclaiming that God's glory extends throughout the heavens and the earth. He then goes on to say that despite God's loftiness, He is still intimately involved in the life of man, and continually bestows good upon him. The Psalmist uses three examples to express the good that God does: (1) He raises the needy from the dust; (2) He seats them with the nobles; and (3) He transforms the barren woman into a joyful mother of children.

How do these three examples of God's kindness encapsulate all the good that He does for mankind?

The Torah tells us that God has three distinct relationships

---

1. This chapter presents only a taste of Maharal's great commentary on *Hallel*.

with humanity, and that all that He does is a manifestation of one of these three relationships. They are kindness, judgment, and mercy.[2]

Everything that happens to us, whether good or bad, and everything that God gives us, whether a lot or a little, comes via one of these three relationships. Realizing a $10,000 profit on a financial investment, for example, is not a random occurrence; it is because God has decided to give it to us for one of three reasons: (1) There was no reason for us *not* to receive it, and God's nature is to bestow good upon us (the relationship of kindness); (2) we deserve it (the relationship of strict judgment); (3) although we were unworthy to receive it, God saw that we needed it and gave it to us anyway (the relationship of mercy).[3]

It was to these three qualities that King David was referring in the first psalm of *Hallel*.

"He raises the needy from the dust..."

Here King David is praising God for doing something that *should* be done. It is not right for poor people to wallow in the dust; shelter should be provided for them. When God cares for the destitute, He is relating to man through the attribute of judgment, or fairness.

"To seat them with the nobles, the nobles of His people."

When King David says that God seats the needy with the no-

---

2. The commentaries derive this from the verse, *"I am your God, I do kindness, judgment, and charity (mercy) in the land"* (*Yirmeyahu* 9:23). *Gevuros Hashem*, chapter 62. See also Ramchal, *Da'as Tevunos* 190.

3. Every Shabbos morning, in the *Nishmas kol chai* prayer, we recite: "He runs His world with *kindness*, His creations with *mercy.*" The commentators explain the meaning as follows: The world as a whole can be directed by God with kindness, as there is often no reason for it not to receive God's goodness. Individuals, however, have often done wrong, and have therefore created a reason for themselves *not* to receive good. They can only be given sustenance via the relationship of mercy.

bles, he is praising God for doing a kindness for man that goes above and beyond fulfilling man's basic needs. Raising a poor person out of poverty may be just, but elevating him to a position among princes is an act of great kindness.

"He transforms the barren woman into a joyful mother of children."

When God gives a barren woman children, it is not an act of "judgment," as "judgment" would have events transpire exactly as they are physically able to act. The barren woman is not capable of having children, and would not conceive. Neither is it an act of kindness, as having children is a function of human beings and not "above and beyond" humanity's basic needs. Rather, allowing a barren woman to conceive and give birth is an act of mercy. Even though this woman is unable to have children naturally, God still allows her to conceive and bear children.

And so, in this chapter of *Hallel*, King David is saying: Praise God for relating to man in three unique ways, and for using each one of them to bestow blessing upon him![4]

B'tzeis Yisrael

When Yisrael went out of Egypt, the house of Yaakov from a people of a strange language; Yehudah became His sanctuary, and Yisrael His dominion. The sea saw it, and fled; the Jordan was driven back. The mountains skipped like rams, the hills like young sheep. What ails you, O sea, that you flee? O Jordan, that you are driven back? You mountains, that you skip like rams...? Tremble, you earth, before the presence of the Lord, before the presence of the God of Yaakov, Who turned the rock into a pool of water, the flint into a fountain of waters.

The praises of the second psalm of *Hallel* (*Tehillim* 114) continue where the praises of the previous one leave off: While the first chapter praises God for the three ways He relates to humanity

---

4. *Gevuros Hashem*, chapter 62.

within the normal realm of the natural world, the second, *B'tzeis Yisrael*, praises God for things He does that transcend nature, that are miraculous.

* * *

"The sea saw it, and fled. The mountains skipped like rams, the hills like young sheep."

When describing the reaction of the physical world to the revelation of God through His miracles, King David begins by noting the reaction of the water.

Water has no shape of its own; it takes the shape of its container. As explained in chapter 3, this makes it an extreme *chomer* entity. Similarly, the earth is a quintessential *chomer* entity. Man can manipulate it any way he wants: He can cultivate it to yield produce, or he can consolidate it to form the foundation of a house.

God is the antithesis of *chomer*; He is the ultimate *tzurah* of the world, as He gives form and definition to all His creations.

A *tzurah*'s nature is to imprint a shape, a form, a definition, onto *chomer*, to impose a *tzurah* onto it. Thus, it was natural that the sea "fled," and the mountains "skipped" like young sheep, as soon as they perceived their antithesis (God) approaching.

* * *

"[God] turned the rock into a pool of water, the flint into a fountain of waters."

These words follow in the theme established above. Here, King David praises God as the quintessential *tzurah*, the One Who imprints His will onto creation. A rock is not impressionable. It can only be imprinted upon through great skill and effort — and even then only with the help of a hammer and chisel.

Yet, in relation to God, says King David, even rock is *chomer*. As with water and earth, He shapes it effortlessly.[5]

---

5. *Gevuros Hashem*, chapter 62.

Lo Lanu

Not to us, God, not to us, but to Your Name give glory, for Your steadfast love, and for Your truth. Why should the nations say, Where is now their God? Our God is in the heavens: He has done whatever He has pleased. Their idols are silver and gold, the work of man's hands. They have mouths but they cannot speak, eyes they have but they cannot see, they have ears but they cannot hear, noses they have but they cannot smell, they have hands but they cannot feel, feet they have but they cannot walk, nor can they speak through their throat. They who make them are like them; so is everyone who trusts in them.... God is their help and their shield.

While the first chapter of *Hallel* praises God for the kindness He does for humanity within nature, and the second chapter speaks about the miracles God does for humanity that defy nature, this third psalm (*Tehillim* 115) addresses the *reason* that God performs miracles for the Jews.

King David compares the abilities of man with the abilities of idols, and finds idols ridiculously lacking.

In the human body each and every organ and limb performs a unique function. An idol, in contrast, has a perfectly formed body, but is incapable of even the most basic functions. The idol has a mouth, which seems molded for speech, yet is mute. Its ears have a shape perfectly suited for hearing, but it is deaf. In fact, none of its organs carry out the functions for which they were intended.

The basic tenet of idol-worshipers is that God's Presence enters their idols and infuses them with spirituality. Yet, if the idol's organs do not work, the idol is a lacking, flawed object.

Is it rational to assume, asks King David, that the Complete and Whole God would rest His Presence in inherently incomplete vessels?

* * *

In the above chapter, King David mentions a number of abili-

ties that man has, but that idols do not have:
- The ability speak (mouth)
- The ability to see (eyes)
- The ability to hear (ears)
- The ability to smell (nose)
- The ability to feel (hands)
- The ability to walk (feet)
- The ability to make sounds (throat)

The significance of the order in which these abilities are mentioned is this: King David begins by describing the most important ability that man has, and moves down to his least significant ability.[6]

The first ability that King David mentions is speech. The power of speech (i.e. man's ability to think intelligently and then express his thought) is most essential in man. So important is the power of speech that the first time the word "man" is used in the Torah (*"Let us make man,"* Bereshis 1:26), the commentary Unkelos defines man as "a spirit that speaks."[7]

Sight is mentioned second because it is the farthest-reaching ability of man. A person can see a vast number of things simultaneously. Quantitatively, one can relate most to the physical world

---

6. Of course, the most essential component of man is his mind, his thought itself. King David does not mention "they have heads but do not think" because he is contrasting the *abilities* of man with the *abilities* of idols. *Thinking* is what man *is*, not an ability that he *has*.

7. Note that the physical ability to speak, developmentally, is closely related to the level of intelligence. A newborn baby, who does not have any knowledge of language, does not say words at all. A toddler, who understands the world on a simple level, is able to articulate words and sentences. As a child grows and develops intellectually, his vocabulary and powers of expression expand. An adult, who has a full mature intelligence, has the full-fledged power of speech (*Gevuros Hashem*, chapter 64).

by means of sight.

Hearing is the next far-reaching capability of man. The ear can hear sounds that originate at great distances, although not as far away as he can see.

The ability to smell is mentioned next. The sense of smell also extends beyond the body: Man can smell something that is quite far away from him, although not as far away as something he can hear or see.

The ability to touch is the next most significant ability that man has. Although it is limited to that which is close to the body, touch still allows man to relate to things outside of himself. Although touch is not as far-reaching as smell, it still gives man the ability to relate to the world around him.

The ability to walk is next. One's legs do not directly relate him to the world in the way that his hands do; they merely enable him to move from place to place.[8]

Creating sounds (as opposed to speech, which is the communication of thought) is considered the least "far-reaching" ability that man has. Generally, a person's actions are enacted through an obvious series of muscle movements. The creation of sound, however, takes place inside the body, and requires very little muscle action visible to the eye.

And so, says King David, idols are inherently flawed. They have perfect forms, but are absolutely powerless. They cannot perform a single human function — from the most significant (speech) to the least significant (sound).

Therefore, it is wholly inconceivable that God, Who is the epitome of Wholeness, would have rested in them and imparted spirituality into their incomplete forms![9]

Hashem Z'charanu

Hashem will bless our remembrance: He will bless the house of

---

8. Similarly, the feet are not nearly as sensitive to touch as are the hands.
9. *Gevuros Hashem*, chapter 64.

Yisrael; He will bless the house of Aharon. He will bless those who fear God, both the small and the great. May God increase you more and more, you and your children. May you be blessed of God, Who made heaven and earth. The heavens are the heavens of God: but He has given the earth to the children of man. The dead cannot praise God, nor can any who go down into silence. But we will bless God from this time forth and for ever more. Hallelukah!

This paragraph is the second half of the 115th psalm. The previous paragraph ended with the words "God is...their shield." Praising God for being our "shield" is recognizing that He protects us from harm — a passive form of beneficence. In this paragraph, King David praises God for His *active* kindness to us, beginning with "Hashem will bless our remembrance."

* * *

The above verse seems unclear. Why should God give blessing to our *remembrance*? Isn't that a distant form of blessing? Why not give blessing to *us*?

A person's "remembrance" means much more than any other aspect of him. It means the lasting impact he has on others, which is much more meaningful than just his name or his face. Many people whom he has affected during his lifetime may forget his name, but the impression he made on them will remain with them forever.

Therefore, it is of great significance that God blesses our "remembrance." God is saying that the lasting impact we have on others, and on the world, will be a blessing!

* * *

"The dead cannot praise God, nor can any who go down into silence."

Indeed, it is only when a person is alive that his existence "proclaims" the glory of God. When a mass of a few hundred organs combine with bone and muscles to work in unison, forming human beings who can walk, talk, see, hear, think, feel, and relate to the world — this speaks of a Creator Whose greatness is Divine.

The brain looks like an unassuming piece of muscle matter. Its ability to organize trillions of bytes of information, and to download pictures, information, and sound in an instant, speaks of brilliance that is unfathomable to a human being. Moreover, the human eye, ear, and all the other parts of the body and its systems are also awe-inspiring.

Similarly, the world in which we live also proclaims its Creator in its every detail. The perfect symmetry and uniqueness of every snowflake speaks of a Master Designer with infinite imagination. The breathtaking scenery of snow-covered mountains and lush green hills, shaded differently each hour of the day, betrays a Master Designer Who can only be Divine.

It is only when the human body and the world at large are functioning properly that they "sing" the praises of God, says King David. A lifeless body, or an earth that is barren or chaotic, would have very little in it that would express God's glory.

And this is King David's prayer: O, God! Allow us to live, allow us to thrive, so that our very existence can proclaim Your glory![10]

Ahavti

I love God Who hears my voice and my supplications. Because He has inclined His ear to me, therefore I will call upon Him as long as I live. The cords of death surrounded me, and the pains of the grave have found me: I found trouble and sorrow. Then I called upon the Name of God; "O Lord I beseech you, deliver my soul." Gracious is God, and just; and our God is merciful. God preserves the simple: I was brought low, and He saved me. Return to your rest, O my soul; for God has dealt bountifully with you. For You have delivered my soul from death, my eyes from tears, my feet from stumbling.

---

10. *Gevuros Hashem*, chapter 64.

* * *

"You have delivered my soul from death, my eyes from tears, my feet from stumbling."

In this spirited chapter of *Tehillim* (116), King David sings his thanks to God for saving him from his enemies, and for relieving his suffering. In expressing his thanks, he notes that God saved his soul from death, his eyes from tears, and his feet from stumbling.

Why does King David limit his thanks to God for these three kindnesses? Should he not have thanked Him for saving his *entire* being from harm?

Perhaps these three things [the soul, eyes, and feet] represent the entire human being.

Indeed, there are three parts of man: his body (or physical side), his soul (or nonphysical side), and his existence as a composite of body and soul, which together form an essentially spiritual human being who can function in the physical world.

When King David thanks God for delivering *"my soul from death,"* he is thanking Him for saving his entire metaphysical side, or soul, from total oblivion.

When he thanks God for saving *"my eyes from tears,"* he is thanking Him for preserving the connection between his body and soul that allows him to continue living. How do the eyes represent the connection of body and soul?

The eyes are unique among the parts of the body. They are encased within a physical body, and can only observe things in the physical world. Yet they cannot actively enter into the world the way the arms and legs can. In this way, they represent a mixture of the physical and nonphysical, and parallel the connection between the body and the soul within man.[11]

When King David thanks God for saving *"my feet from stum-*

---

11. While usually the third item mentioned represents the combination of the first two, "my eyes from tears" is mentioned second for a reason explained in footnote 12.

bling," he is thanking Him for saving his body, his physical component. Why do the feet represent the physical aspect of man? A person's feet are at the bottom of his body, where his body touches the ground. Because the feet connect man to the physical, *chomer* earth, they represent the physical aspect of man.

* * *

Let us now decipher the second half of the three phrases cited above, where King David tells us what he was saved *from*.

The first and third phrases are easily understandable: King David praises God for saving his soul from death, clearly the most significant potential loss; likewise, he praises Him for preventing his feet from stumbling, a most commonplace occurrence.

The second phrase, however, is not as readily understood. Why does King David thank God for saving his eyes from *tears*, and not from blindness, the most significant potential loss from that organ?

Tears are closely related to the soul. When the energy that is created in one's soul (its passion, hopes and longings) builds up to a point where it can no longer be contained in the body, it spills out as tears. When a person cries, it is as if part of his soul has poured out. The loss of tears is more significant than the hurt of any other part of the body because it represents a loss of part of the soul.[12]

Mah Ashiv

How can I repay God for all of His kindness to me? I will carry the cup that You have filled with salvation, and call upon the Name of God. I will pay my vows to God now, in the presence of all His people.... I will offer to You the sacrifice of thanksgiving, and I will call upon the Name of God. I will pay my vows to God

---

12. *Gevuros Hashem*, chapter 64. That is why "my eyes from tears" is placed between "my soul from death" and "my feet from stumbling."
Rabbi Shimshon Raphael Hirsch calls tears "the sweat of the soul."

in the presence of all His people, in the courts of God's House, in your midst, O Yerushalayim, Hallelukah!

* * *

"I will carry the cup that You have filled with salvation, and call upon the Name of God."

The analogy of a cup being filled is used to capture a specific image. It is as if King David is saying that he had always "held a cup," and now "his cup" has been filled. He had always known that he had a body — an empty vessel that had the potential to be "filled" with meaningful accomplishments. Now, he thanks God for filling his cup, as he sees that he has been given the ability to act in great ways.

* * *

"I will carry."

The use of the word "carry" is very significant. There are two ways that a person can transport something: in his arms or on his back. When the object is in his arms, the object becomes apparent (to a person facing him) before he himself is seen. If the object is on his back, however, he is seen before the object.

That is what King David is saying: O God: I will carry the cup that You have filled for me "in my arms," in a way that it will be the first part of me that people will encounter. The cup that You have filled will precede me; I will use it to proclaim Your greatness.

* * *

"I will pay my vows to God in the presence of all His people."

This verse continues with the same theme. King David is saying here that the vows he made in private, he will fulfill to God in public; his mission is to use every possible opportunity to proclaim the greatness of God, to use his every ability to publicly honor God's glory.

Hodu Lashem[13]

O give thanks to God for He is good, for His kindness endures forever. Let Yisrael now say, that His kindness endures forever. Let the house of Aharon now say, that His kindness endures forever. Let those who fear God now say, that His kindness endures forever.

The Hebrew root of the word "to thank" (*Hodu*, הודו) also means "to agree" or "to concede." The meanings are interconnected: To the extent that a person recognizes and acknowledges that God has given him all that he has, he is moved to thank Him for His benevolence.

It follows, then, that different people, who have experienced the beneficence and closeness of God on different levels, will sing the praises of God differently, corresponding to their respective experiences. In this chapter of *Tehillim* (118), King David notes four levels of praises to God, each on a higher level than the previous one.

He opens with a general statement: "O give thanks to God for He is good, for His kindness endures forever." All of humanity, says King David, ought to thank God for the good He does in the world.

In the second sentence, King David addresses the Jewish People. The Jewish People have a relationship with God that is much closer and more comprehensive than the relationship of the rest of the world with God. Therefore, King David says, "Let Yisrael now say, that His kindness endures forever." The Jews experience God more deeply than do the other nations, and therefore must praise God on a higher level.

In the third sentence, King David addresses the *Kohanim*. The *Kohanim* were a privileged group who served in the Temple and were immersed in an atmosphere of closeness to God, unparal-

---

13. The ideas throughout the rest of this chapter are taken from *Gevuros Hashem*, chapter 64.

leled in everyday life. They were as close as anyone could be to God's Presence in this world, and therefore had an even deeper understanding of God. King David, thus, compels them to sing their own praise of God, on an even higher level than that of the rest of the nation.

In the last sentence of this section, King David calls upon "those who fear God" to praise Him.

People who truly fear God, who have a constant, all-pervasive awareness of His Presence, have a deeply profound connection with Him. They experience God's omnipresence with their emotions and physical senses as well as intellectually. It is natural that these people would express their praise of God on a level commensurate with their experience. Thus, King David says to them: Your understanding of God is the deepest and most profound of all. You too, offer your praise of God!

Min Hameitzar

Out of my distress I called upon God, God answered me with liberation.... All the nations surrounded me but in the Name of God I cut them off. They surrounded me, indeed they surrounded me, but in the Name of God I cut them off. They surrounded me like bees, they were quenched like a fire of thorns, for in the Name of God I cut them off.

In three consecutive sentences King David describes his enemies' attacks on him. In the first sentence he says "All the nations (my enemies) surrounded me." In the second sentence he repeats this expression twice. In the third he says "They surrounded me like bees," describing an even more serious assault.

King David is telling us that he suffered three levels of attack from his enemies. He is also telling us that those three levels represent the levels of hatred. If a nation dislikes other nations because they are different, the dislike is magnified in the case of the Jews. The Jewish People have endured from their enemies throughout history.

The first verse, which says "All the nations surrounded me" once, refers to a basic level of dislike. This is natural; every nation is wary of its neighbors, because they are potential economic, cultural, and even military threats. No nation likes seeing its neighbor becoming too dominant or successful.

The second verse (which repeats the verse "they surrounded me" twice) alludes to a deeper level of hatred. A nation dislikes other nations because they are different and therefore a threat. This is magnified in the case of the Jewish People. The Jews have a totally different value system from the rest of the world — one that is absolute and based on the word of God. Morally, they are as different as could be from the other nations, whose value systems are subjective and self-serving. If the *un*like is *dis*liked, then it is clear why the Jews suffer such intense dislike from the nations of the world.

In the third verse, King David uses a terrifying analogy of being surrounded by a vicious swarm of enemies ("They surrounded me like bees") to describe an even more drastic level of enmity. This subtle but deep-seated hatred has its roots in the subconscious mind, where the nations recognize the spiritual power of the Jewish People. They are aware, on some level, that their success is dependent on the Jews' failure.

If the Jews act in accordance with their spiritual potential, and do God's will, the world's events will be centralized around them for their benefit. But if the Jews do not live their life in accordance with God's will, they will be punished, and the fortune of the world will lie in the hands of the nations. There is a "seesaw" of power, and only one of the two can be on top at any given time.

The nations hate the Jews, then, much as one despises a rival who, he knows, can overtake him at any moment.

Hallelukah
"*O praise God, all you nations...*"

The word "*Hallelukah*" is a compound of two words: "*hallelu*" (praise) and *"kah"* (God).

Hallelukah is unique in the Hebrew language in that it is the only word in the Hebrew language that combines a word of praise with a name of God. There are many other words that praise God, but they do not contain a Divine name within them.

Interestingly, the word *Hallelukah* is used largely for one category of God's actions — the miraculous. Why is this?

The Talmud teaches that God effected the creation of the world through the spiritual energy contained within two letters. This world was created with the letter ה (*hei*), and the world to come was created with the letter י (*yud*). These two letters comprise God's name of י-ה (*"kah"*), which in turn represents God's natural order in the world.

That is the meaning of the word *Hallelu-"kah."* By praising the One Who created the world with the letters י and ה, we are saying that He — and only He — can suspend those rules at will, and disrupt the order of nature to perform miracles when He sees fit.[14]

Addendum: "One Who Says Hallel Every Day"

The Talmud says (*Shabbos* 118b), "One who reads the *Hallel* every day curses God." What is the meaning of this statement? Why is saying *Hallel* every day a negative thing?

One who says *Hallel* every day is praising God for being the ultimate controller of the world, One Who can change its natural order at will. Once a person appreciates God's omnipotence, he expects to see God reward the good deeds of the righteous and punish the sins of the wicked, immediately and decisively. The repetitive saying of *Hallel* strengthens this conviction.

This is problematic for the following reason:

During the forty years that the Jewish People spent in the desert, they had an unparalleled relationship with God and He

---

14. While we do find some things that God does within the natural world that are praised with the word *"Hallelukah,"* anything that God has done outside of nature is praised *only* with the word *"Hallelukah."*

responded immediately to their actions. The perpetrators of the golden calf were punished instantly with a deadly plague. The *misonanim* (those who complained about the food in the desert [*Bemidbar* 11:1]) were also punished immediately with a devastating plague. On the other hand, the Jews were rewarded instantly with two spiritual crowns when they said, regarding the acceptance of the Torah at Sinai (*Shemos* 24:7), "We will do and then we will hear" (*Shabbos* 88a).

After their entry into the Land of Israel, however, a more "natural" mode of operation was set into motion. Dramatic miracles were no longer the norm, and God did not always punish the wicked or reward the righteous right away — often not even in their lifetimes.[15]

One who says *Hallel* every day continuously asserts that God relates to us openly and with miracles. However, our current reality is not that way. We do not always see the righteous receive reward and the wicked punishment. He who recites *Hallel* every day therefore brings this incongruity to mind.

Asking the question of why the righteous suffer and the wicked prosper is not considered to be praise of God. It raises a difficulty that may be resolved in our minds, but not in our hearts. This does not strengthen our will to serve God with all our heart and soul. And this is why the Talmud says that a person who says *Hallel* every day has "cursed God."

---

15. God prefers this more concealed relationship with man because He wants the world to operate in a "natural" way, one which would allow man free choice to believe in God or (God forbid) not. If miracles were everyday occurrences, and actions met with immediate reward or punishment, man would be *forced* to acknowledge God.